New Directions for
Adult and Continuing
Education

Susan Imel
Jovita M. Ross-Gordon
COEDITORS-IN-CHIEF

MW01221955

Class Concerns
Adult Education
and Social Class

Tom Nesbit
EDITOR

Number 106 • Summer 2005
Jossey-Bass
San Francisco

CLASS CONCERNS: ADULT EDUCATION AND SOCIAL CLASS
Tom Nesbit (ed.)
New Directions for Adult and Continuing Education, no. 106
Susan Imel, Jovita M. Ross-Gordon, Coeditors-in-Chief

Microfilm copies of issues and articles are available in 16mm and 35mm, as well as microfiche in 105mm, through University Microfilms Inc., 300 North Zeeb Road, Ann Arbor, Michigan 48106-1346.

NEW DIRECTIONS FOR ADULT AND CONTINUING EDUCATION (ISSN 1052-2891, electronic ISSN 1536-0717) is part of The Jossey-Bass Higher and Adult Education Series and is published quarterly by Wiley Subscription Services, Inc., A Wiley company, at Jossey-Bass, 989 Market Street, San Francisco, California 94103-1741. Periodicals Postage Paid at San Francisco, California, and at additional mailing offices. POSTMASTER: Send address changes to New Directions for Adult and Continuing Education, Jossey-Bass, 989 Market Street, San Francisco, California 94103-1741.

SUBSCRIPTIONS cost $80.00 for individuals and $170.00 for institutions, agencies, and libraries.

EDITORIAL CORRESPONDENCE should be sent to the Coeditors-in-Chief, Susan Imel, ERIC/ACVE, 1900 Kenny Road, Columbus, Ohio 43210-1090. e-mail: imel.l@osu.edu, or Jovita M. Ross-Gordon, Southwest Texas State University, EAPS Dept., 601 University Drive, San Marcos, TX 78666.

Cover photograph by Jack Hollingsworth@Photodisc

www.josseybass.com

CONTENTS

Editor's Notes

Social class is a major determining factor of accomplishment in most educational, employment, and social arenas—still one of the best predictors of who will achieve success, prosperity, and social status. Yet class is difficult both to define and discern. We can examine it empirically only through its consequences or outcomes. Thankfully, educational systems are so central to the functioning of advanced industrial societies that they provide fertile ground for the investigation and analysis of class.

Education closely influences personal and social development in the technical and economic spheres but also in the wider political arenas of emancipation and democracy. Education also affects how people experience social, cultural, and economic forces; and it shapes abilities and dispositions toward their transformation. Because of this, education has always represented a site of struggle between those with the power to define what constitutes legitimate knowledge and those excluded from such decision making.

These aspects of education are closely related to issues of social class. Ideas about class influence the goals and purposes of education, its forms and approaches, as well as where and when it takes place and who participates in it. Class not only affects these elements but also shapes how we think about them. At its most fundamental level, the goal of education—and particularly adult education—is usually to ameliorate the social disadvantages of learners' backgrounds; yet too often education serves only to further extend such differences. So it's ironic that, compared to the related analytic vectors of gender and race, class is so unexplored in North American adult education. Why do scholars acknowledge class so significantly less than its counterparts? Why is it so underrepresented in social and educational theory? Indeed, why does American society generally so abjure or ignore class? And what might adult educators do about it?

This sourcebook addresses these questions by exploring the role of class in various areas of adult education policy and practice. Its purpose is less to provide an exhaustive examination of all aspects of class than to introduce key themes, topics, trends, and approaches. Examining the operation of class in this way helps clarify how class informs the interrelated roles of structure and agency in our work as adult educators. It also explains how adult education practices produce, reproduce, and maintain the complex inequalities of social class across varied contexts. The goal is to help adult educators better appreciate how values and purposes are inherent in their educational work and how larger social structures and norms influence adult educators and their work. Thus, the sourcebook encourages readers to observe and comprehend the role of class in shaping their own conceptions about and practices of adult education. Because the focus is firmly on practice, this volume also encourages readers to explore how they might increase their students' and colleagues' awareness and understanding of class and class analysis and how they might strengthen these aspects in their own teaching and research.

Because class is understood and appreciated differently around the world, the sourcebook tries to highlight such diversity in approach by deliberately involving authors from several different countries: Australia, Canada, England, Scotland, South Africa, Sweden, and the United States. As well as being able to provide an international perspective, the authors are all strong advocates for class analyses and practices that champion the less privileged. Each author is not only an experienced scholar and practitioner of adult education but also a committed social activist. So their chapters depart from the conventional academic practice of examining class through a dispassionate academic lens or viewing it from the standpoint of middle-class culture (which tends to regard the working class adversarially).

Each chapter assumes a slightly different focus in exploring how class shapes a specific area of adult education practice. In Chapter One I provide a historical overview of the development of the concept of class and its applicability to the study of adult education. The following two chapters deal with the macro and micro aspects of class and adult education. In Chapter Two Kjell Rubenson explores how social class has influenced the development of social policies about adult education in various countries. He argues that the present policy discourse on adult education is a result of weakening working-class interests. Then in Chapter Three, Lyn Tett explores learning and identity through the analytic lens of social class. Showing how assumptions about learner identity are often based on a deficit view of the working classes, she illustrates an alternative discourse that shows how to generate useful knowledge in a family literacy program.

The next three chapters all recognize that adult education activities have to take place in specific arenas and communities of practice. In Chapter Four Griff Foley examines the role of educational institutions in supporting working-class learning. In asserting that a distinctive working-class learning style exists, Foley analyzes the institutional educational experiences of working-class adults and shows how they can suggest approaches that are supportive, challenging, and class-conscious. In the following chapter on the pedagogical influences of social class, Janice Malcolm considers how class helps construct the identity and ultimately the teaching of certain groups of educators. She also explores ways of making class explicit within teacher education classrooms. In Chapter Six Shirley Walters examines how class influences the educational activities of social movements. Drawing on examples from her native South Africa, she illustrates how class, intertwined with other social categories, fundamentally shapes the organizational and educational practices of social movements.

Thinking about class draws attention to other forms of oppression. People's experiences of class also depend on their race and gender, so no meaning of class is completely independent of such factors. The next two chapters explore the intersections and interweavings of class, gender, and race in greater detail. In Chapter Seven Mechthild Hart focuses on gender. She describes how women's labor is beneficial to global capitalism and thus how class and gender are inseparable, regardless of the specific national or cultural content in which women work. In Chapter Eight Shahrzad Mojab examines the dialectical relationship between class and race as it pertains to adult education epistemology, pedagogy, and practice. Finally, in Chapter Nine I summarize some of the key ideas about social class, discuss their continued relevance to the work of adult educators, and identify some further resources.

Acknowledgments

Over the years many people have helped me think about the relationships between social class and adult education. I'm honored that several have either contributed to this sourcebook directly or appeared in the reference lists. Others, not included here but nevertheless influential, include (in chronological order) Richard Hoggart, Robert Noonan, Les Roy, Sarah Harrop, John Berger, Michael Standen, Simon Henderson, C.L.R. James, John Stirling, Doug Gowan, Janet Ericsson, Richard Ross, Adrienne Burk, John Hurst, Phyllis Cunningham, Budd Hall, Libby Tisdell, Mike Welton, Peter Jarvis, Fred Schied, Gunilla Härnsten, D'Arcy Martin, Jack O'Dell, and Nick Blomley. I also want to thank Susan Imel, who supported the idea of this sourcebook so enthusiastically and offered many practical suggestions; Jovita Ross-Gordon, the model of a careful but compassionate editor; and Ed Taylor, with whom I discussed some of the initial ideas and who, as always, has been a constant source of support and encouragement. Some of these folks I know personally; a few are even good friends; others I know chiefly through their work and writing. Yet I want to acknowledge each by name because they constitute a group of colleagues with whom I share a (too often unspoken) sense of solidarity; being able to work alongside them is a privilege. To me they represent a class of adult educators committed to the struggle for social justice through the development of a democratic and critical practice of teaching adults. *La lutta continua.*

Tom Nesbit
Editor

TOM NESBIT is director of the Centre for Integrated and Credit Studies and associate dean of continuing studies at Simon Fraser University in Vancouver, British Columbia.

1

The author introduces the importance of class, providing a historical overview of the concept and discussing its applicability to the study of adult education.

Social Class and Adult Education

Tom Nesbit

Economic, social, and cultural factors profoundly influence how we live and what we do. The societies we live in, the relationships we have and create with other people, the ways we accommodate or resist unfairness and oppression, and the ways we choose to think about these phenomena are both limited and enabled by our place in the economic structure of society. Whether we like it or not, at individual, community, and societal levels, everything we believe and everything we do is influenced by our place in an economic and social order. So education, like all other areas of social activity, operates within a set of social, cultural, and economic relations and is shaped by cultural and economic influences (Althusser, 1971; Gramsci, 1971).

Education also shapes how we experience social, cultural, and economic forces. It's through education that we first come to understand the structures of society and the ways that power relations permeate them. Educational systems are thus one of the most important vehicles for *hegemony*, the process by which a society inculcates and maintains dominant ideas by portraying them as natural and normal. Because of this, groups and individuals regularly use the systems, institutions, policies, approaches, and practices of education to perpetuate positions of privilege and power. Two ways to do this are to favor technical rather than emancipatory knowledge and skills (Habermas, 1972) and to socialize people into accepting particular economic systems and cultural traditions. In doing so, dominant groups reproduce existing patterns of social relations and reinforce unequal distribution of power and privilege. Ironically, the education system also legitimates its role in social reproduction by deflecting attention away from the process. However, education can also counter hegemony by helping people understand how they might resist and challenge social structures and by suggesting ways to do so.

These relations establish the environments in which adult educators work. As Habermas (1972) also indicated, adult education is a moral and political endeavor as much as it is a technical practice, and it is thus affected by its role in maintaining or challenging the social order. Do adult education policies and practices reproduce existing relations of dominance and oppression? Alternatively, do they contribute to social as well as personal change? Answering such questions involves exploring the extent to which adult educators acknowledge notions of class and the related demands of capitalist ideology.

Capitalism seems a far cry from the common situations and interactions of adult educators, yet capitalist ideas are so insidious and pervasive that they affect every aspect of our work. Capitalist societies commodify human activity by subjecting all aspects of peoples' lives and social relations to market requirements. These relations are then normalized and made to seem natural. In capitalist societies, our prestige and status is related to productive ability; society values us by how much we earn. Such basic aspects as where we live, how we earn a living, who our friends are, and what access we have to healthcare and education are all dependent on our ability to produce wealth and other resources. Of course, these attributes are not fixed permanently; because the distribution of resources is unequal, people strive to maintain or enhance their own share. Thus, people's struggle for access to and control of resources is dynamic. Capitalist societies are stratified into *classes*, hierarchies of power and privilege related to the ownership and control of various forms of capital. Capitalist systems of structured inequality continue because society portrays them as normal or inevitable: the system encourages its victims to blame themselves for their failure to be successful. In this way dominant groups are able to maintain the status quo and the hegemony of their own ideas without facing too strong a challenge from those less powerful.

So understanding the relationships between class and educational policies and practices is important to a full appreciation of adult education. In this introductory chapter, I outline these various relationships. I first distinguish some ideas about class and then explore how they inform educational practices in general. Next, in focusing specifically on discussions of class in adult education, I chart the ground for the remaining chapters to explore in greater detail.

What Is Class?

Although Aristotle identified the segmenting of society by economic, social, and cultural distinctions, the concept of class is fairly recent. Its present use dates from mideighteenth-century France. At that time the *Encylopédistes,* a group of intellectuals who sought to assemble all available knowledge, developed a systematic classification first of plants, animals, minerals, and natural phenomena and then of the social and economic positions of people in society (Seabrook, 2002).

The concept of class later gained wider currency with the industrial revolution and the changes it brought about. By the midnineteenth century, Marx was using class as the foundational concept for explaining social organization in terms of understanding the ownership, means, and control of work processes and material wealth (Marx and Engels, [1845] 1970). He claimed that societies consisted of two classes: the bourgeoisie (which owned and controlled the mills, mines, and factories) and the proletariat (workers with little more than their labor power to sell). The relationship between these two classes is essentially unequal, exploitative, and beneficial mainly to the bourgeoisie. Those who own capital reinvest their profits to earn even more; those who don't must sell their ability to work in order to survive. Wealth thus returns to the owners, and workers perpetuate their own dependence. That is, though the working class generates surplus wealth, it does not equally profit from it. Because the bourgeoisie own the means of production and distribution of resources, that class disproportionally appropriates and accumulates wealth.

As modes of production and types of work became more complex, many came to regard the division of society into two opposing classes as overly reductionist and outmoded. Industrial societies shifted from a principally manufacturing basis toward the inclusion of more service- and knowledge-based industries. Forms of work became more elaborate and thus confounded existing notions of class. Intermediate class positions developed, and European societies soon settled into the now more familiar structuring of three classes—upper, middle, and lower, though these are still largely related to occupation and income. Most recently the concept of a fourth class, an underclass, has arisen. This rather unfortunately named group consists of those whom society considers outside of or largely excluded from the established economic order, such as the certifiably insane, the long-term unemployed, drug addicts, recent immigrants, prisoners, and others with certain so-called pathological deficiencies who are significantly dependent upon state welfare (Morris, 1994).

Of course, the explanatory and analytic power of class as a concept relates more to the notion that society is still stratified in ways that link individuals and groups with the economic order of production than it does to the specific number of different classes, their definition, or even the people who form them. So whether there are two, three, four, or even more classes, every division of society by class continues to stigmatize the less well-off and to define them as responsible for their own demise. Class still exists. As in Marx's time, all social life continues to be marked by the struggles and conflicts over access to the generation and distribution of wealth and status.

Not everyone regards class in such materialistic terms. Weber ([1920] 1968), for instance, argued that class is better defined by also including notions of culture, values, politics, and lifestyle. People who fall within the same economic class may nevertheless occupy different social-class positions and have differing opportunities for acquiring work, earning income, developing skills, obtaining education, and owning property. For Weber one's class is based more on these life chances, cultural background, status, and life outside of work than on one's relationship to the ownership and control of the means of production. Rather than see society as a two-class system, Weber posited a system of social stratification of many different classes that sometimes overlap. Classes need not be formally organized along such rigid lines. In other words, people from similar backgrounds need not communicate directly with one another in order to maintain their lifestyle, status, and prestige. In essence, they can act in concert without organizing themselves to do so.

This less-deterministic approach is also visible in the work of Bourdieu, for whom a class is any grouping of individuals sharing similar conditions of existence and tendencies or dispositions (Bourdieu and Passeron, 1977). Equally important as one's location in an economic order is the possession of various forms of capital—economic, cultural, social, or symbolic—that can constellate differently in different societies. Bourdieu's concept of class thus takes into account other stratifying factors, such as gender, race, ethnicity, place of residence, and age. Finally, these class structures are not predetermined or imposed from without but more subtly reproduced. For example, people with like dispositions can discriminate (often unwittingly) against those who have different lifestyles and personal characteristics. Note that both Weber and Bourdieu allow more scope for human agency than did Marx but still regard external class structures as fundamental and quite constant. In other words, class relationships transcend the individuals who occupy the positions: people may move around or stay put, but society is still structured along class-based axes of inequality and exploitation.

These two broad views have shaped the development of the concept of class in European and North American countries. In Europe, throughout the social upheavals of industrialization, older ideas of rank continued to affect definitions of class. The so-called lower orders, the laboring classes, and the middling ranks of society (such as merchants or teachers) existed alongside the aristocracy and the gentry. However, as the stratification of industrial society became less rigid, these definitions settled into the more familiar classification of working, middle, and upper class. Most recently, scholars have recognized that this depiction treats class as essentially static. Although it underlines the fundamentally economic nature of class, such a definition ignores the dynamic and shifting nature of the relationships between those who possess wealth and power and those who do not. Class has now come to be regarded more as a relation that is constantly changing. As British historian Thompson (1968, pp. 9–10) puts it, "class is not a category . . . but rather an historical relationship between one group of people and another. . . . It is defined by men [sic] as they live their own history."

North American countries—which, since colonization, have largely developed in response to European feudalism—see themselves as relatively free from such archaic categories as aristocracy and the lower orders. Especially in the United States, one commonly hears that class has ceased to exist or that everyone is middle class. For Zweig (2000, p. 4), class is one of the nation's best kept secrets; any serious discussion of it is "banished from polite company." Instead, the ethics of self-reliance and mobility and the ideologies of individualism, egalitarianism, and meritocratic achievement have been more powerful forces than class solidarity. Nowadays existential rather than social factors tend to influence who Americans think they are. For example, it is far more common for people to define themselves as black, gay, Jewish, Latino, lesbian, or mobility-challenged than to refer to themselves in terms of class.

One of the so-called successes of capitalist ideology has been to reinforce the notion that individual identity is unrelated to such supposedly hidden forces as class. Identity politics (commonly based on individualistic claims of importance) represent the success of this misconception. Identity and other subjective politics (usually less overtly opposed to capitalism) are also more readily comprehensible and therefore more appealing. So even though vast institutionalized social inequalities persist in the United States, the discussion of class remains relatively ignored. Scholars tend to discuss social stratification more in terms of identity, inequality, or status rather than of opposing social classes. Paul Fussell (1992, p. 18) describes class as the "dirty little secret" of the United States, for, when compared with such categories as race or gender, class appears invisible. Of course, it's precisely this invisibility that, when linked with its apparent naturalness, allows an unfair class system to reproduce itself continually. Ironically, even though people might not discuss class much, it still remains a subjectively relevant category in their minds. Studies repeatedly indicate that, when asked, people have little difficulty placing themselves into a class and identifying strongly with it (Beeghley, 2000).

Given these different perspectives and ambiguities about class, examining it can often be difficult. Wright (1979) identifies four major approaches to understanding class: a functional differentiation of positions within a society, groups unified by their common position in a hierarchy of power or authority, groups with different market capacities that result in different life chances, and a shared location in the social organization of production. However, whatever one's orientation, an attention to class and class analysis reveals several general principles. First, a class analysis focuses on materialist concepts regarding the production and reproduction of social life and the importance of human activity in shaping both material subsistence and consciousness. Second, a class analysis highlights the fundamental and dynamic relationships between economic and social structures; the ideologies that frame our world; and the ways we experience, understand, and shape the world. Third, a class analysis suggests that we cannot explain social phenomena by their surface manifestations nor by the ways that individuals experience them but as, instead, representations of external divisions of power. Fourth, a class analysis provides a basis for explaining why people organize themselves into collective forces to resist injustice and exploitation. Finally, for those with a commitment to social justice, a focus on class also raises several important questions: How do we negotiate or internalize dominant ideologies and relations of ruling? How might alternative ones develop? How can marginalized people, silenced by social, economic, and cultural relations of power, recover their voices and the right to be heard? Because we can address these questions educationally, I now turn to exploring the relationships between class and education.

Class and Education

Education is meant to inculcate dominant values, not confront them. Because educational institutions are generally a middle-class domain, their policies and practices are weighted strongly in favor of middle-class values. So capitalist societies, in which class operates as the primary structuring of social inequality, usually ignore or bury class perspectives. As such, many adult educators are uncertain about how their work reflects underlying political structures, let alone economic systems. Observing the effects of power and privilege is far easier than determining their causes. Yet a number of studies explore how education reproduces existing patterns of power. Economists Bowles and Gintis (1976) demonstrated how educational systems are part of a system of broader capitalist class relations. Their correspondence theory explains how, in general, schools reproduce the social relations that capitalist production requires. As Bowles and Gintis describe, capital requires two things: workers of specific types and relative social stability and ideological acceptance of class relations. The capitalist class thus has a broadly shared set of interests pertaining to educational systems and the capacity to promote such interests.

Some find the correspondence theory too mechanistic or reductive; it allows little agency for those involved. One less-deterministic approach came from Bourdieu (Bourdieu and Passeron, 1977) who suggested that education serves the interests of the privileged by structuring learners' access to and uses of various forms of social and cultural capital. Others have introduced notions of struggle and resistance into this process. Most notably, Willis (1977) showed how several working-class teenage lads consciously resisted and rebelled against school and classroom authority. Tellingly, however, this resistance worked better within school than outside it: when the lads left school, they remained unable to find anything but unskilled and unstimulating jobs. The work of McLaren (1995) and Apple (1996) also shows how individuals can resist and contest social and cultural oppression in educational settings. They document the complex relationships between cultural reproduction and economic reproduction and explore how class interrelates with the dynamics of race and gender in education.

All these studies indicate the essential role of education in promoting and maintaining the social relations required for capitalist production. Further, they suggest that we can fully understand education only as part of a broader capitalist class system. Although we now recognize that the relationships between educational practices and political structures are much more complex than correspondence theory suggests, adult educators who work in such areas as Adult Basic Education, literacy, vocational education, and the pernicious welfare-to-work programs will recognize how often their work, the policies about it, and the textbooks and curricula they use are still much more closely tied to employers' needs than to their adult or working-class students' interests (D'Amico, 2004; Kincheloe, 1999; Livingstone, 1999; Rose, 1989).

Focusing on Adult Education

Adult education is not divorced from these trends. Together with K–12 and higher education counterparts, it is now firmly established as central to the smooth functioning of economic systems and societies. As such concepts as lifelong learning and the knowledge society gain prominence, education and training become key vehicles for preparing people to be adaptable to economic changes in society. Even though the aim of adult education is generally to ameliorate the social disadvantages that class and background produce, nowadays adult education often serves to exacerbate those disadvantages.

Despite this, scholars have left social class and its effects relatively underexplored, especially in North American adult education. For example, although ideas of class clearly inform several of the contributions to the two most recent editions of the *Handbook of Adult and Continuing Education* (Merriam and Cunningham, 1989; Wilson and Hayes, 2001), overall, the handbooks treat the topic only tangentially. Further, when we compare studies of class with the related analytic vectors of gender and race, we see that scholars do not explore class so rigorously. Recent ERIC searches combining the descriptors *adult education* with *gender, race,* and *social class* produce totals of 531, 322, and 85 hits, respectively. Assuming that the number of ERIC references roughly correlates with researchers' interests, why do researchers acknowledge class so significantly less than its counterparts? Why is class so underrepresented in social and educational theory? Why is it ignored as the elephant in the room (hooks, 2000)?

Of course, some adult educators have addressed issues of class more overtly. Most of the North American studies contained in the ERIC database focus on the consequences or experiences of class and explore such issues as the participation, access, and attainment of different groups. In documenting how social class affects participation in adult education programs, those studies consistently underscore how far social class remains a key determinant of adult participation in organized learning. To give just one recent example, Sargent and Aldridge (2002) indicate that upper- or middle-class adults are twice as likely to engage in some sort of learning activity than are those from the working class.

However, although they detail that class is a major factor affecting adult education participation, most studies in the ERIC database do not really explore how class works. From a conceptual perspective, they add little to London's classic study (London, Wenkert, and Hagstrom, 1963, p. 3, which explored the important contribution that adult education makes to larger society, specifically for those deemed "less educated and less skilled." London and his colleagues found a strong connection between social class and people's abilities to prosper in a rapidly changing world. Class not only affected participation in adult education activities but also was closely related to such other facets of social life as jobs, vocations, and leisure pursuits. Anticipating the subsequent debates about lifelong learning, London's report called for adult education and training to "become a continuing part of everyone's life" (p. 148), providing "both education for work and education for leisure" (p. 153).

This concentration on the results rather than the causes of class is perhaps understandable. Individuals tend to internalize the conflicts within hierarchical systems, especially those individuals without much power. Also, people usually closely experience class at the same time as other, more recognizable forms of oppression. These factors, when combined with the scarcity of class scrutiny, ensure that people do not always have readily available concepts to identify—let alone analyze—the class aspects of their experiences. So scholars continue to overlook class in the theoretical lexicon.

Thankfully, some adult educators have taken up the challenge of making class more explicit. In recent years North American scholars Collins (1998), Livingstone (1999), Sawchuk (2003), Schied (1993), and Welton (1995) have each provided sophisticated and complex analyses of class by examining the dynamic relationships between it and the associated practices, policies, and discourses of adult education. Elaborate explorations of class and adult education are more prevalent abroad. In addition to the authors of the following chapters, Allman (2001), Freire (1985), Stromquist (1997), Thompson (2000), Westwood and Thomas (1991), and Youngman (2000) all provide rich empirical and theoretical studies that tie adult education practices to class and the increasingly globalized nature of capitalism. Discussions of adult education and social class are also available outside of the traditional adult education literature; the concluding chapter of this sourcebook suggests some further examples and provides a more extensive reading list. Finally, because the authors of subsequent chapters come from different geographic areas and foci of interest, their reference lists also contribute to a comprehensive resource for further study.

Summary

Although social class is rarely evident in adult education discourse, no one should doubt its existence. All adults know that life chances and social opportunities differ greatly. Some are born into illiterate families; others into households fit around shift work, seasonal employment, or poverty. Others are raised with enough money, mobility, and access to feel encouraged and engaged. Economic sufficiency deeply affects all manner of human experience. And access to education remains the best hope for most adult learners, regardless of class, to secure economic stability and become more fully engaged citizens—a concern that lies at the heart of most adult education policies and practices. Because of this and specifically because of the general lack of awareness of class issues, adult educators should strive to find ways to discuss it. Regardless of individual political orientation, all adult educators need to find ways to link individual experiences with their social causes. Such persistent examination can help develop what some have called a sociological imagination—the ability to see the connection between the immediate, individual experience and societal, complex structures (Mills, 1967). In capitalist societies this means understanding the power and reach of social class. Though we commonly hear that class has largely disappeared, continuing to accentuate it helps us resist and challenge what Allman (2001, p. 209) has called the postmodern condition: "skepticism, uncertainty, fragmentation, nihilism, and incoherence." It can also provide an antidote to the social amnesia, self-absorption, and apolitical theorizing that pervades much of current adult education discourse.

References

Allman, P. *Critical Education Against Global Capitalism. Karl Marx and Revolutionary Critical Education.* New York: Bergin & Garvey, 2001.

Althusser, L. "Ideology and Ideological State Apparatuses." In B. Brewster (ed.), *Lenin and Philosophy.* London: New Left Books, 1971.

Apple, M. W. *Cultural Politics and Education.* New York: Teachers College Press, 1996.

Beeghley, E. L. *The Structure of Social Stratification in the United States.* Needham Heights, Mass.: Allyn & Bacon, 2000.

Bourdieu, P., and Passeron, J. C. *Reproduction in Education, Society, and Culture.* Thousand Oaks, Calif.: Sage, 1977.

Bowles, S., and Gintis, H. *Schooling in Capitalist America.* New York: Basic Books, 1976.

Collins, M. *Critical Crosscurrents in Education.* Malabar, Fla.: Krieger, 1998.

D'Amico, D. "Race, Class, Gender, and Sexual Orientation in Adult Literacy: Power, Pedagogy, and Programs." In J. Comings, B. Garner, and C. Smith (eds.), *Review of Adult Learning and Literacy,* vol. 4: *Connecting Research, Policy, and Practice.* Hillsdale, N.J.: Erlbaum, 2004.

Freire, P. *The Politics of Education: Culture, Power, and Education.* New York: Bergin & Garvey, 1985.

Fussell, P. *Class: A Guide Through the American Status System.* New York: Touchstone, 1992.

Gramsci, A. *Selections from the Prison Notebooks.* (Q. Hoare and G. N. Smith, trans. and ed.) New York: International, 1971.

Habermas, J. *Knowledge and Human Interests.* Portsmouth, N.H.: Heinemann, 1972.

hooks, b. *Where We Stand: Class Matters.* New York: Routledge, 2000.

Kincheloe, J. L. *How Do We Tell the Workers? The Socioeconomic Foundations of Work and Vocational Education.* Boulder, Colo.: Westview Press, 1999.

Livingstone, D. W. *The Education-Jobs Gap.* Boulder, Colo.: Westview Press, 1999.

London, J., Wenkert, R., and Hagstrom, W. O. *Adult Education and Social Class*. Berkeley: University of California, Berkeley Survey Research Center, 1963.

Marx, K., and Engels, F. *The German Ideology*. (C. J. Arthur, trans. and ed.) London: Lawrence and Wishart, 1970. (Originally published 1845.)

McLaren, P. L. *Critical Pedagogy and Predatory Culture*. New York: Routledge, 1995.

Merriam, S. B., and Cunningham, P. M. (eds.). *Handbook of Adult and Continuing Education*. San Francisco: Jossey-Bass, 1989.

Mills, C. W. *The Sociological Imagination*. New York: Oxford University Press, 1967.

Morris, L. *Dangerous Classes: The Underclass and Social Citizenship*. London: Routledge, 1994.

Rose, M. *Lives on the Boundary: The Struggles and Achievements of America's Underprepared*. New York: Free Press, 1989.

Sargent, N., and Aldridge, F. *Adult Learning and Social Division*. Leicester, England: National Institute of Adult Continuing Education, 2002.

Sawchuk, P. H. *Adult Learning and Technology in Working-Class Life*. New York: Cambridge University Press, 2003.

Schied, F. M. *Learning in Social Context*. DeKalb, Ill.: LEPS Press, 1993.

Seabrook, J. *The No-Nonsense Guide to Class, Caste and Hierarchies*. Oxford: New Internationalist Publications, 2002.

Stromquist, N. P. *Literacy for Citizenship*. Albany, N.Y.: SUNY Press, 1997.

Thompson, E. P. *The Making of the English Working Class*. Oxford: Oxford University Press, 1968.

Thompson, J. *Women, Class and Education*. New York: Routledge, 2000.

Weber, M. *Economy and Society: An Outline of Interpretive Sociology*. (G. Roth and C. Wittich, eds.; E. Fischoff, trans.) New York: Bedminster Press, 1968. (Originally published 1920.)

Welton, M. R. *In Defense of the Lifeworld: Critical Perspectives on Adult Learning*. Albany, N.Y.: SUNY Press, 1995.

Westwood, S., and Thomas, J. E. (eds.) *Radical Agendas? The Politics of Adult Education*. London: National Institute of Adult Continuing Education, 1991.

Willis, P. *Learning to Labour: How Working-Class Kids Get Working-Class Jobs*. Farnborough, England: Saxon House, 1977.

Wilson, A. L., and Hayes, E. R. (eds.). *Handbook of Adult and Continuing Education (New Edition)*. San Francisco: Jossey-Bass, 2001.

Wright, E. O. *Class Structure and Income Determination*. San Diego, Calif.: Academic Press, 1979.

Youngman, F. *The Political Economy of Adult Education*. London: Zed Books, 2000.

Zweig, M. *The Working-Class Majority*. Ithaca: Cornell University Press, 2000.

TOM NESBIT *is director of the Centre for Integrated and Credit Studies and associate dean of continuing studies at Simon Fraser University in Vancouver, British Columbia.*

2 *Social class has strongly influenced the development of social policies about adult education. Present policy discourses are a result of weakening working-class interests.*

Social Class and Adult Education Policy

Kjell Rubenson

Historically, the development of adult education has been closely linked with the aspirations of the working class. In the early 1900s, adult education served as intellectual weaponry in the struggle for political rights and improved working conditions. In the 1960s adult education started to become a concern for the state. This interest was to a large extent driven by the first wave of human capital theory and a growing awareness of the injustices of a hierarchical school system that had diminished the life chances of many adults. At the policy table, labor unions tried to influence government policies to become more responsive to working-class interests and aspirations. By 2004 a concern for human resources development and the fostering of individual learning, all in a spirit of lifelong learning, have broadly replaced these aspirations. As adult educators, we have to ask: Why are there drastic cuts in public funding of adult literacy and Adult Basic Education programs? How can policymakers in North America, as in many other parts of the world, repeatedly talk about the necessity of developing the skills and competences that individuals need in order to be productive citizens in the knowledge economy and then quickly turn around and decide that unemployed workers need only a short training course? And why have we put our trust in market forces for producing the education that we need to handle the challenges that rapid social and economic changes have set?

A fundamental assumption in this chapter is that the changes we have been observing in adult education policies are a consequence of a reduced capacity in organizing political opposition to the influence of the capitalist class. As Korpi (1983) points out, the difference in power resources in a society between major collectives or classes, particularly capital and organized labor, regulates the distribution of life chances, social consciousness, and conflicts on the labor market. According to Korpi, the more developed the organizing capacity of the labor movement, the more developed the welfare state will become.

In this chapter I will address how the present policy discourse on adult education is a result of weakening working-class interests. The discussion will start with a brief review of the debate on the breakdown of class politics. Following this, the chapter turns to broader trends in policies of adult education.

The Breakdown of Class Politics

In their 1991 article, Clark and Lipset suggested that changes in social relations of the economy, political parties, and family had resulted in a decline of the importance of social class. They point to a diminishing of class members voting as a bloc and the changes in party platforms. The former is central because elections traditionally have been the platform of the democratic class struggle (Niuwberta, 2004). Niuwberta's analysis reveals that a decline of the manual labor force has driven a substantial decline in class voting in the postwar period in almost all democratic countries.

Lipset (2004) notes the changes in the party platforms of the European left parties, which have increasingly become socially and ideologically pluralistic. In order to secure enough votes to become the ruling party, they have chosen to appeal more to the expanding middle stratum and not concentrate exclusively on the left's traditional base, industrial workers and the poor. Following in the footsteps of New Labour in the United Kingdom, so-called Third Way social democrats have been stressing free-market policies and smaller government while promoting welfare policies that encourage independence. Instead of nurturing the traditional link between unions and the political party, the New Left has tried to distance itself from this alliance.

Pakulski (2004) makes a crucial point when he notes that accepting a decline of the influences of class does not in any way imply the end of capitalism, the disappearance of social stratification, a reduction of social inequality, the abating of social conflicts, or finally, the "end of social" or declining relevance of political sociology (p. 139). Instead, he maintains that the weakening of working-class organizations, particularly large trade unions that have been the core organizations striving for class identification, consciousness, solidarity, and political behavior among workers, will result in an increase in inequalities. Replacing the traditional class-based politics is, according to Pakulski and others, a rise of new politics that involve new value preferences; new issues and concerns; new political culture with more direct involvement; new institutional forms, including the new social movements; and new social bases. What drives this shift is a postmaterialist worldview that prioritizes quality of life, self-fulfillment, and civil liberties. Pakulski notes that politics tends to become specialized and issue-centered in its response to a population that is increasingly being differentiated by educational attainment and skills, gender, generation, ethnicity, and sexual preferences.

Similarly, Beck and Beck-Gernsheim (2002) observe that an apparent contradiction surrounds the reality of classes in advanced societies. Although structures of social inequality display a surprising stability, society in general no longer perceives or politically handles questions of inequality as questions of class. We can find the explanation in Beck's analysis (1992) of the individualization process that has accompanied the evolution of the risk society during the last three decades. Beck and Beck-Gernsheim (2002) draw attention to how the German welfare state brought people a relatively high standard of living and social welfare that freed them from traditional class and resulted in the dissolution of lifeworlds associated with class- and status-group subcultures. The expansion of education is central in this process because education makes possible a certain degree of self discovery and reflection. According to the authors, as the common risk of becoming unemployed increasingly stretches across groups defined by income or education, it has become less and less possible to relate the development of forms of solidarity in society to the historical model of the proletarian productive worker. Consequently, trade unionist and political modes of action now compete with individually centered legal and medical or psychotherapeutic remedies and compensations. Beck and Beck-Gernsheim stress that this value system of individualization is embedded in a new ethics that is based on the principle of duty to oneself. Unlike many social commentators, they maintain that this development is not an expression of egoism and narcissism. Instead, it is about a new focus on self-enlightenment and self-liberation as an active process for individuals to accomplish in their own lives, including the search for new social ties in family, workplace, and politics. With the individualization processes gaining in strength, the authors believe that the traditional class society will become insignificant beside an individualized society of employees. When trying to address social problems, people no longer will organize along a class model but seek temporary coalitions with different groups and camps, depending on the particular issue at stake.

Global Trends

The global trends that this chapter describes reflect to a large degree the situation in North America. The discussion will focus on how to understand these changes in the context of global capitalism driving a neoliberal agenda that emphasizes individual economic responsibility rather than reliance on state welfare and the broad developments toward a second phase of modernity in which society is increasingly characterized by individualization processes.

As the industrialized world struggles to adjust to mounting economic and social pressures, adult education has shed its marginal position and evolved as a central policy issue. Lifelong learning is a key element of the economic and social strategy that the European Council adopted for the first decade of the new century (European Union [EU], 2000). Lifelong learning has also penetrated the Organisation for Economic Co-operation and Development (OECD), which in its first forty years more or less neglected adult education. It was therefore a notable event when, at the end of 1998, the OECD Educational Committee launched its thematic review of adult learning (OECD, 2003).

Two major interrelated developments are shaping the current debate on adult education policy: (1) an erosion of the social contract and (2) a changed relationship between education and the economy. In the late 1970s, the political consensus that had guided government spending on welfare-state programs began to shift (Richards, 2000). The global policy agenda was grounded on a neoliberal ideology with an emphasis on shrinking the Keynesian welfare state and freeing the market. The privatization trend that cut across most OECD countries during this period required the transfer of costs and responsibility from public or state control to private control. The neoliberals maintain that not only does the nation-state lack the power to resist global economic forces but also that it better serves its citizens' well-being if the country opens up to international market forces (Johnson, McBride, and Smith, 1994).

In this climate the utopian ideas on lifelong education that the United Nations Educational, Scientific and Cultural Organization (UNESCO) presented in the early 1970s did not meet with the approval of neoliberal governments. Following the 1972 Fauré report, *Learning to Be,* UNESCO's Institute for Education concentrated its policy and research effort on lifelong education. The concept was one of personal development, with the emphasis on people *making themselves* rather than *being made.* An important issue in the analysis was how a system of lifelong learning could reduce rather than increase educational gaps in society. In some aspects the discussions appear as almost a preamble to today's preoccupation with individualization. The expectation is that through self-evaluation, self-awareness, and self-directed learning, humans will work toward achieving the central goals of democracy, humanism, and the total development of self. However, Fauré's report also presented in utopian terms an awareness of structural issues and a deep-rooted search for the necessary democratic conditions. The report repeatedly stressed that a crucial weakness in societal structures is an absence of political will, not only toward the democratization of education but also toward the democratization of society.

Consequently, the existing social relations of production were seen to provide a major obstacle to the true realization of lifelong learning; indeed, lifelong learning will become a new arena for social struggle because it will require a classless society (Vinokur, 1976). The 1970s discussion on lifelong education and lifelong learning became a strange mixture of global abstractions, utopian aspirations, and narrow practical questions and remained at the level of vague ideas; a different paradigm that reflected the new political economy later replaced that discussion.

In an era of what Thurow (1996) calls global capitalism, characterized by increased economic competition and rapid advances in information technology affecting the structure of the labor market as well as individual jobs, the policy debate on lifelong learning centered almost exclusively around an economistic worldview. The EU's white paper on education and training (1996, p. 1) typifies the situation when it states: "The basis of the white paper is the concerns of every European citizen, young or adult, who faces the problem of adjusting to new conditions of finding a job and changes in the nature of work. No social category, no trade is spared this problem."

To better understand the educational discourse that both the OECD and the EU promoted and replicated in North America and Australia, it is essential to note that the new agenda on lifelong learning was driven not only by an economistic position but also by a neoliberal framework that had replaced the Keynesian creed.

Adult education and training, like education in general, was to become responsive to labor-market needs (OECD, 1989). This was part of an active labor-market policy aimed at getting the growing number of unemployed people off welfare and into the labor market. As Crouch, Feingold, and Saco (1999) point out, encouraging education seems to have been a way for many political parties to evade certain welfare commitments while offering governments opportunities for constructive and positive action. Increasingly, government policies linked welfare and social assistance programs to individuals' willingness to work and their readiness to undertake some form of labor-market training program to enhance their employment prospects. Skills training programs should focus on getting clients job ready, and welfare policy should promote short welfare-to-work programs. This training would be quite distinct from the training for highly skilled jobs, because skilled jobs and unskilled jobs exist in quite separate labor markets.

With economic relevance becoming the key concept driving government policies on adult education and training, business interests became primary. The business sector had the lead role in defining what competencies and skills the public adult system should produce. The state actively intervened with the purpose of promoting closer ties between adult education providers and business and industry. Working-class interests had little influence in a policy climate of general suspicion of the state and a belief in the greater efficiency of free-market forces.

Toward the end of the 1990s, policymakers had come to the insight that although the new economy holds the promise of increased productivity and an improved standard of living, it also introduces a new set of transitions and adjustment challenges for society, industry, and individuals. Unmet, these challenges could increase the permanent exclusion or marginalization of segments of the population and exacerbate socioeconomic divisions. The new understanding in policy circles came to affect the discourse on lifelong learning and resulted in a softening of the economistic perspective. The EU memorandum (2000) signals that a shift had started to take place. The document, reflecting on decisions from the 2000 Lisbon European Council, departs from the assumption that contemporary social and economic change are interrelated and stresses two equally important aims for lifelong learning: promoting active citizenship and promoting employability. The document states that the "EU must set an example for the world and show that it is possible both to achieve dynamic economic growth and to strengthen social cohesion. Lifelong learning is an essential policy for the development of citizenship, social cohesion and employment" (p. 4).

Recognizing market failures and growing concerns about large groups not participating fully in social and economic life, the third generation is a shift in balance between the three institutional arrangements. The market still has a central role, but the responsibilities of the individual and the state are also visible. The language is one of shared responsibilities. However, a closer reading of the text and the understanding that seems to dominate the present policy debate might lead one to be more skeptical of what looks to be a major shift in the public discourse on lifelong learning. Despite the repeated reference to the involvement of all three institutional arrangements, what stands out in recent policy documents is the stress on individuals' responsibility for their own learning—something that the documents underscore time after time. Recognizing that EU member states are responsible for their education and training systems, the 2000 document—as well as later ones—points out that these systems are dependent on the input and commitment of a wide range of actors from all walks of social and economic life. However, with special emphasis on the individual, the EU paper (p. 4) states, "and not the least upon the efforts of individuals themselves, who, in the last instance, are responsible for pursuing their own learning."

Thus, a fundamental assumption in the present discourse on lifelong learning is that lifelong learning is an individual project. Individuals become responsible for making adequate provision to create and preserve their own human capital. Investment in learning and its financing then becomes primarily an individual responsibility (Marginson, 1997). The stress on the individual responsibility closely mirrors New Labour's so-called Third Way program, which has come to have a profound influence on the policy platform of European social democratic parties. The Third Way, although advocating an understanding of the good society and promoting a balance between state, market, and civil society, reflects the hegemonic influence of neoliberal thinking on left-leaning governments (Ryner, 2002). Reflecting its underlying philosophical ethos, Giddens (2000, p. 165) states, "the precept 'no rights without responsibilities' applies to all individuals and groups. . . . Government must maintain a regulatory role in many contexts, but as far as possible it should become a facilitator, providing resources for citizens to assume responsibility for the consequences of what they do." The heightened emphasis on the individual's responsibility for his or her own learning is closely embedded in a changing understanding and articulation of the very concept of lifelong learning and is a move away from a preoccupation with education to a focus on learning (Griffin, 1999; Rubenson, 1999).

Within the European Employment Strategy (an EU policy on job creation that links it closely with lifelong learning), the member states have defined *lifelong learning* as "all purposeful learning activity undertaken on an ongoing basis with the aim of improving knowledge, skills and competence" (EU, 2000, p. 3). But to what extent is it possible to approach policy on lifelong learning fruitfully from such a broad understanding of the concept?

The uncertainty of the state's role is evident in the EU's progress report on the follow-up to its 2000 resolution on lifelong learning (EU, 2001). First, the member states have little or no legislation specifically on lifelong learning. Instead, it continues to appear mainly as a general principle underlying various separate education and training policy reforms. Second, the EU is vague on how to finance continuing education and training. Third and most problematic, the EU member states' policies on lifelong learning hardly address workplace learning. Their progress report makes many general references to the role of social partners but makes little specific mention of their role in stimulating participation and innovation in lifelong learning. It does not note the fact that very unequal learning opportunities exist for skilled and unskilled labor. What the EU policy discussion seems to forget is that for most of its citizens the opportunities for organized forms of adult learning have become closely linked to work. Thus, in the EU member countries as in North America, more than half of the participants in adult education and training attend an employer-supported activity (OECD, 2000). Consequently, if the state wants to engage seriously with the issue of lifelong learning for all and ways to equalize opportunities for adult education and work, it has to consider "the long arm of the job" (Rubenson, 2003, p. 26). However, only in trade union documents can one find any direct mention of individual rights of access to lifelong learning and the suggestion that governments and employers should conceive and guarantee workers' right of access in terms of time and resources (see, for example, European Trade Union Confederation, 2001).

Workers do not seem to be part of policymakers' definitions of target groups for lifelong learning. Instead, following Beck and Beck-Gernsheim's individualization thesis (2002) we can notice that present-day policy documents present and address inequality not as a class question but in terms of various at-risk groups (migrants, ethnic minorities, refugees, and those lacking information, communication, and technology skills, to mention the most commonly identified populations). In this respect most policy documents bear clear witness of the new politics and post-Fordist production politics that this chapter discussed earlier.

A closer review of the EU progress report (2001) reveals that the Nordic countries in particular have structures in place to help those not participating in adult education to overcome psychological and institutional barriers. These include outreach measures for those least likely to participate spontaneously in adult education and training as well as financial aid for this group. Programs in other countries offer much less concrete proposals for the disadvantaged.

I will argue that we can explain the differences between adult education policies in Sweden and most other European countries and those in Canada and the United States by the differences in welfare-state regimes. Thus, when we try to understand the formation of adult learning in a time of economic and social challenges, it is important that the Nordic welfare state, founded on working-class political power, is still in place, with its institutional arrangements and traditions. Four elements in the Nordic welfare state have profound effects on adult education.

First, the Nordic welfare-state model has been associated with an active labor-market policy. Consequently, thinking about human capital has influenced not only the special labor-market training programs but also reforms in adult education generally (Rubenson, 2003). In accordance with the Nordic welfare-state model, recent reforms offer quite extensive education and training to the unemployed (often three years of general programs). The Nordic adult education strategy is an instrument in what some call a high-road strategy to economic competitiveness, resulting in a virtuous circle of high skills, high productivity, and high wages (Wong and McBride, 2003). The opposite is a low-road strategy, which assumes a bifurcated labor market with a high-skill sector containing so-called good jobs and a large sector of low-pay, low-skill jobs. The latter tends to encourage the state to promote adult education training programs as part of welfare-to-work schemes, which offer short-term, low-end programs. Although this issue has yet to arouse much debate in U.S. adult education literature, Bok (2004), Schultz (2000), and Soni (2004) all provide stimulating discussions on welfare reforms in the United States (such as the 1998 Workforce Investment Act) and their implications for lifelong learning.

Second, the Nordic tradition of industrial relations, with its developed corporatist structure, has fostered a tradition of collaboration between the state and labor-market organizations. Norwegians Dolvik and Stokke (1998) argue that contrary to common assumptions, globalization will undermine national corporatism and that the Norwegian example suggests that renationalized cooperative practices can be a viable strategy for coping with such pressures. This has helped develop a comparatively high degree of consensus on issues like productivity, the introduction of new technology, and training (Qvale and Øverland, 2001). The central involvement of trade unions in adult education, at all levels of the organization, helps adult education become part of a worker's individual and collective identity.

Third, in contrast to the situation in most other countries, Nordic countries have a publicly supported sector of popular adult education that partly can balance the strong economistic tendencies in adult education policies.

Popular adult education can be a part of the corporate state, lying at the cross-roads between civil society and the state. The state will subsidize popular adult education because it wants to support an enterprise that aims to make it possible for people individually and collectively to influence their position in life and promote commitment to participate in society's development.

Fourth, a funding regime is one of the key policy instruments available for influencing participation in adult education. The Nordic tradition ear-marks funding for target groups, and this tends to compensate for the increased costs involved in recruiting the underprivileged. In a time when government policies in many countries seek to increase efficiency by adopt-ing a more market-oriented approach and outcomes-based funding, the Nordic model provides an example of an alternative funding regime that lessens the likelihood that employers seek those easiest to recruit and more likely to succeed (see McIntyre, Brown, and Ferrier, 1996).

It is important to note that the drive toward individualization, as out-lined by Beck and Beck-Gernsheim (2002), has not escaped the Nordic wel-fare-state regime. Thus, in a fundamental shift from the traditional social democratic position on adult education, a recent government bill from Swe-den (2000) stresses that the individual's needs must be the starting point for planning social measures. The bill notes that adult education and training has so far been too concentrated on treating the individual as part of a col-lective with a common background and common needs. Therefore, the chal-lenge for state-supported education and training is to cater to every individual's wishes, needs, and requirements. Although the language of the Swedish reform bill strongly resembles the global ideas, note that the dis-course is different from the neoliberal one in that the state is clearly a player. The state allocates resources for outreach activities, counseling, availability of courses, and financial support as the base of a state-supported infra-structure for lifelong learning.

Concluding Note

The brief review of adult education policy tends to support Clark and Lipset's (1991, 2004) thesis that broader social and economic changes have diminished the influence of class politics on adult education policy. How-ever, all surveys on participation in adult education and training clearly reveal that this has in no way diminished the great inequities in who enrolls. The OECD's international literacy survey (2000) manifests that people who are already well educated and have high-skill jobs are the citizens of the knowledge society. However, the document also suggests that working-class interests still have a profound impact on adult education and training poli-cies, particularly in the Nordic countries, and that the nation-state still is central in determining access to learning opportunities.

The lack of a working-class interest in the political project on lifelong learning is paradoxical in view of the well-documented centrality of work in the everyday living of lifelong learning. I would therefore argue that, contrary to some of the critics of present developments in adult education policy (see, for example, Banal, 2000; Gustavsson, 2002), the main threat to the utopian project of adult education may not be that an economic rationale so strongly drives public policy on adult education but that the political project on adult learning has lost its link to economic democratization. Instead, a progressive political project on lifelong learning must reestablish this connection. This will demand that working-class forces can break the present trend, which, in the words of Beck and Beck-Gernsheim (2002), is making the class society insignificant besides an individualized society of employees.

References

Banal, R. "Lifelong Learning and the Limitation of Economic Determinism." *International Journal of Lifelong Education,* 2000, *19*(1), 20–35.
Beck, U. *Risk Society: Towards a New Modernity.* London: Sage, 1992.
Beck, U., and Beck-Gernsheim, E. *Individualization.* London: Sage, 2002.
Bok, M. *The Job Training Charade.* Thousand Oaks, Calif.: Sage, 2004.
Clark, T. N., and Lipset, S. M. "Are Social Classes Dying?" *International Sociology,* 1991, 6(4), 397–410.
Clark, T. N., and Lipset, S. M. (eds.). *The Breakdown of Class Politics: A Debate on Post-industrial Stratification.* Baltimore: Johns Hopkins University Press, 2004.
Crouch, C., Feingold, D., and Saco, M. *Are Skills the Answer? The Political Economy of Skill Creation in Industrial Countries.* New York: Oxford University Press, 1999.
Dolvik, J. E., and Stokke, T. A. "Norway: The Revival of Centralized Concertation." In R. Hyman and A. Fermer (eds.), *Changing Industrial Relations in Europe.* Oxford: Blackwell, 1998.
European Trade Union Confederation (ETUC). "Lifelong Learning Trade Union Strategy." Resolution adopted by ETUC Executive Committee, June 13/14, 2001. [see http://www.peretarres.org/eutses/recursos/bolonya/4_Doucuments_dels_agents/05_DOCA_ETUC.pdf]. Accessed March 1, 2005.
European Union (EU). *Teaching and Learning: Towards the Learning Society.* Brussels: European Union, 1996.
European Union (EU). *A Memorandum on Lifelong Learning.* Brussels: European Union, 2000.
European Union (EU). *National Actions to Implement Lifelong Learning in Europe.* Brussels: European Union, 2001.
Fauré, E. *Learning to Be.* Paris: United Nations Educational, Scientific and Cultural Organization, 1972.
Giddens, A. *The Third Way and Its Critics.* Cambridge, England: Polity Press, 2000.
Griffin, C. "Lifelong Learning and Social Democracy." *International Journal of Lifelong Education,* 1999, *18*(4), 329–342.
Gustavsson, B. "What Do We Mean by Lifelong Learning and Knowledge?" *International Journal of Lifelong Education,* 2002, *21*(1), 13–23.
Johnson, A. F., McBride, S., and Smith, P. J. (eds.). *Continuities and Discontinuities: The Political Economy of Social Welfare and Labour Market Policy in Canada.* Toronto: University of Toronto Press, 1994.
Korpi, W. *The Democratic Class Struggle.* London: Routledge & Kegan Paul, 1983.
Lipset, S. M. "The Decline of Class Ideologies: The End of Political Exceptionism." In T.

N. Clark and S. M. Lipset (eds.), *The Breakdown of Class Politics.* Baltimore: Johns Hopkins University Press, 2004.

Marginson, S. *Markets in Education.* St. Leonards, England: Allen & Unwin, 1997.

McIntyre, J., Brown, A., and Ferrier, F. *The Economics of ACE Delivery.* Sydney: BACE, 1996.

Niuwberta, P. "The Democratic Class Struggle in Postwar Societies: Traditional Class Voting in Twenty Countries, 1945–1990." In T. N. Clark and S. M. Lipset (eds.), *The Breakdown of Class Politics.* Baltimore: Johns Hopkins University Press, 2004.

Organisation for Economic Co-operation and Development (OECD). *Education and the Economy in a Changing Society.* Paris: OECD, 1989.

Organisation for Economic Co-operation and Development (OECD). *Literacy in the Information Age.* Paris: OECD, 2000.

Organisation for Economic Co-operation and Development (OECD). *Beyond Rhetoric: Adult Learning Policies and Practices.* Paris: OECD, 2003.

Pakulski, J. "Class Paradigm and Politics." In T. N. Clark and S. M. Lipset (eds.), *The Breakdown of Class Politics.* Baltimore: Johns Hopkins University Press, 2004.

Qvale, T. U., and Øverland, E. "Norway—Out of Europe?" In G. Szell (ed.), *European Labour Relations,* vol. 2: *Selected Country Studies.* Aldershot, England: Gower, 2001.

Richards, J. "The Social Contract in a Knowledge Society." In K. Rubenson and H. Schuetze (eds.), *Transitions to the Knowledge Society.* Vancouver: UBC Institute for European Studies Research, 2000.

Rubenson, K. "Adult Education and Training: The Poor Cousin. An Analysis of OECD Reviews of National Policies for Education." *Scottish Journal of Adult Education,* 1999, 5(2), 5–32.

Rubenson, K. "Adult Education and Cohesion." *Lifelong Learning in Europe,* 2003, 8(1), 23–31.

Ryner, M. J. *Capitalism Restructuring: Globalisation and the Third Way.* London: Routledge, 2002.

Schultz, J. H. "The 'Full Monty' and Lifelong Learning in the Twenty-First Century." *Journal of Aging and Social Policy,* 2000, 11(2/3), 71–82.

Soni, V. "From Crisis to Opportunity: Human Resource Challenges for the Public Sector in the Twenty-First Century." *Review of Policy Research,* 2004, 21(2), 157–178.

Sweden. *Government Bill.* Jan. 2000/01:72.

Thurow, L. *The World of Capitalism: How Today's Economic Forces Will Shape Tomorrow's Future.* New York: Morrow, 1996.

Vinokur, A. "Economic Analysis of Lifelong Education." In R. H. Dave (ed.), *Foundations of Lifelong Education.* Oxford, England: Pergamon Press, 1976.

Wong, L., and McBride, S. "Youth Employment Programs in British Columbia: Taking the High Road or the Low Road?" In M. G. Cohen (ed.), *Training the Excluded for Work: Access and Equity for Women, Immigrants, First Nations, Youth and People with Low Income.* Vancouver: University of British Columbia Press, 2003.

KJELL RUBENSON *is professor of educational studies and director of the Centre for Research in Higher Education and Training at the University of British Columbia in Vancouver, British Columbia.*

3

Assumptions about learner identity are often based on a deficit view of the working classes. This chapter illustrates an alternative discourse that shows how one family literacy program in Scotland generated useful knowledge.

Learning, Literacy, and Identity

Lyn Tett

A wide variety of governments and educational bodies currently recognize the value of learning in adulthood through a commitment to policies that promote lifelong learning. These policies aim to develop the individual's capacity for learning across the life span and assume that people can learn in many different ways and contexts. The corollary of these expectations is that if the society that people live in regards learning as a normal activity for people of all ages, then everyone, rather than a limited group, is likely to be effectively engaged in some form of learning of his or her choice. Participation in postschool education and training in the United Kingdom, however, is a highly classed activity. People from the working classes, especially those who are unskilled, low-paid, or unemployed, are unlikely to continue their education; whereas those from the professional and managerial classes are overrepresented, particularly in higher education (see Archer, Hutchings, and Ross, 2003). Because those who leave school with few or no qualifications are unlikely to engage in learning later, even informal learning, it appears that if individuals do not succeed in the first place, they will not succeed later either. Participation in learning is also highly gendered especially in employer-funded education and training for adults, with men receiving a substantially greater share of resources than women (Sargant and others, 1997).

So although we should welcome the commitment of governments to lifelong learning, we must find ways of disentangling the emphasis on economic skill development and individual learning that has permeated these policies. For example, a European Union policy paper (Commission of the European Communities, 2000, p. 5) argued that the aims of lifelong learning "are dependent on [citizens] having adequate and up-to-date knowledge and skills to take part in and make a contribution to economic and social

New Directions for Adult and Continuing Education, no. 106, Summer 2005 © Wiley Periodicals, Inc.

life." The British prime minister, Tony Blair, has similarly argued that "Education is the best economic policy we have" (Department for Education and Employment, 1998, p. 2). Permeating the lifelong learning discourse is an emphasis on the individual, isolated learner and a focus on increasing people's skills and employability.

By emphasizing agency and ignoring the class structures that mediate people's ability to participate in education and learning, this discourse downplays the external forces that affect people. This leads the working classes to assume that lifelong learning is for other people (McGivney, 1990); they often end up being forced to participate in the sort of welfare-to-work programs that emphasize increasing human capital. If education is to enable all people to participate in learning that is their own choice, then we must rethink the focus on skills and employability. Instead, learning should be located in social relationships because this has the potential to engage people in generating new knowledge and ideas from their lived experience (Crowther, 2000).

Adult Literacy Programs

Discussion around adult literacy illustrates the individualizing and class-based discourse of lifelong learning policies very clearly. Thus, the rest of this chapter presents a case study of a literacy program because such programs exemplify dominant approaches and have been the focus of a particularly strong version of the discourse on human capital. Assumptions behind literacy programs are usually that people lack knowledge and are not motivated to learn, so educators must force or encourage them back into participation. Learning is also seen as an individual choice, so society sees adults who have failed to learn the basics as somehow deficient (see Crowther and Tett, 2001). This deficit form of literacy is based on assumptions about people's learning identities that in turn reflect assumptions about how people live out their class in particular ways. It also does not encourage deep learning; rather, it leaves people feeling less confident and capable because it marginalizes their own class-based knowledge.

On the other hand, community-based programs that are grounded in adults' life situations and thus reflect their community's class and culture offer an approach that responds to local issues. If these issues derive from people's own interests and knowledge, they are much more likely to encourage learning that has value for them (see Barton and Hamilton, 1998). This means that rather than seeing literacy and numeracy as the decontextualized, mechanical manipulation of letters, words, and figures, we can instead see literacies as located within the social, emotional, and linguistic contexts that give them meaning. From this perspective reading and writing are complex cognitive activities that integrate feelings, values, routines, skills, understandings, and activities and depend on a great deal of contextual (that is, social) knowledge and intention. For example, someone reading the main news story in a newspaper is not just decoding words but also using knowledge of the conventions of newspaper writing, of the newspaper's local or national focus, and its political and philosophical orientation. In fact, they are reading between the lines. In the same way, adults in a supermarket are not just using number skills when comparing prices but also taking into account their prior experience with the brands, family likes and dislikes, and perhaps ethical concerns (for example, fair trade).

The common way to think about literacy and basic skills at the moment is to see them as rungs on a ladder that people have to climb. Children learn about this ladder at school, and the literacy that adults need is the extension of this process in postschool contexts. The emphasis is therefore on standardizing literacy accomplishments through the use of tests, defining core skills, and aiming for uniform learning outcomes that others specify in advance of the learning process. To define this ladder, proponents construct top-down frameworks largely in terms of prevocational and vocationally relevant literacy requirements. Consequently, they do not recognize the validity of people's own definitions, uses, and aspirations for literacy; such frameworks are disempowering in the sense that they are not negotiable or learner-centered and not locally responsive. They define what counts as real literacy, and they silence everything else.

If we can build on the range of literacy activities that people already engage in and feel comfortable about, then this is one way in which we can positively value the culture of the home rather than seeing it as an inadequate environment for the family's literacy development. Looking at a family literacy project based in an outer-city housing estate in a poor working-class area of a Scottish city will give us an idea of how one might do this (see Tett and Crowther, 1998). By taking a responsive approach to curriculum building, while at the same time positively valuing participants' home and community life, the project sought to include the literacy practices of everyday life in the curriculum and build on them. The project participants were parents of children who attended the area's primary schools; they had identified themselves as having literacy problems that they would like to work on in order to help themselves and their children. Groups of up to twelve, of whom 90 percent were mothers, engaged in the following educational program.

Developing the Curriculum

When they began, the program participants had to identify the literacy practices that they used in the home and community. This revealed a significant range of reading and writing practices that they regularly engaged in but that they easily neglected or considered insignificant. Everyday uses for reading and writing involved, for example, scanning the newspaper's TV pages to find out what was on that day and checking horoscopes. It also involved understanding a range of signs and symbols in the local environment, writing brief notes for family members, making shopping lists, labeling family photographs, keeping note of family birthdays and anniversaries, and sending greeting cards. Recognizing and working on these literacy practices provided an appropriate starting point for the curriculum. This approach based education in everyday literacy concerns and practices and built on what people already knew and did, rather than emphasizing what they could not do. Project staff coupled the approach with a curriculum based on the students' concerns and aspirations about their own and their children's learning and relationships to their teachers. This combination of approaches provided a real incentive for learning because it concentrated on what really mattered to the participants.

Negotiating work in this way was not, however, simply a matter of passing responsibility for developing the curriculum from the tutor to the student, which would be an abdication of tutors' critical, interpretative role. Tutors remained responsible for organizing a pedagogical context in which participants could collectively realize their best potential and in which they all become subjects reflecting together on the process rather than passive individualized objects of the process. The project tutors were also committed to a particular understanding of the nature and purpose of their work that informed their practice. One example was the valuing of home and community literacies and the fostering of effective understanding between home and school literacy practices. So was the way the tutors recognized the potential for others to use family literacy to attribute educational failure to so-called deficit working-class families; instead, this project emphasized the wealth of the knowledge that parents contributed to their children's educational development.

The project staff developed curriculum approaches that built on a range of strategies that supported rather than undermined what parents did. For example, the project staff explicitly encouraged adults to think critically about their own school experiences and worked to avoid simplistic, pathological explanations of failure at school. This involved having participants share their most positive and negative school learning episodes in ways that enabled them to discuss the wide range of experience in the group. This was coupled with student-led presentations that included reflecting on their own experiences of school in ways that problematized their earlier internalized understandings of failure. In addition, participants discussed the differences between their own and their children's school experiences in order to identify changing pedagogical practices. Similarly, project staff urged participants to identify and value their own educative role with their children. This included teaching their children local songs and games as well as talking about daily events. The emphasis was on the positive ways in which parents already successfully educated their children through different ways of knowing the world, instead of assuming that parents lacked knowledge and skills that the teacher had to impart (see Taylor and Dorsey-Gaines, 1988).

Using the Literacy Practices of Everyday Life

This project also sought to include the literacy practices of everyday life in the curriculum, giving a positive value to these working-class participants' home and community life. Students kept a log of their reading and writing practices and also interviewed others about their role as readers and writers in the family. This revealed a significant range of oral communication, reading, and writing practices that people regularly engaged in but easily neglected or considered insignificant—outside as well as within the school.

Recognizing and working on actual literacy practices provided an appropriate starting point for the curriculum because it grounded educational intervention in real literacy concerns and everyday life. This included challenging assumptions about the homogeneity of reading and writing practices because participants revealed through their discussions the wide variation in the group's experiences and the influence of gender, ethnicity, and class on what they considered normal. This then led to a critical examination of the presumptions about family life that their children's reading books contained, revealing assumptions about nuclear family roles that were at odds with many of the participants' own experiences. The next stage of this part of the project was for the participants to create, with the help of the computers, stories for their children that reflected their own lives. Access to good word-processing and drawing programs enabled students to produce attractive texts that were authentic reflections of the relevant issues in their own families and communities.

The project staff also focused on developing critical language awareness through enabling learners to see language and the reading of texts as problematic (see Wallace, 1992). This involved, for example, collecting texts that the participants came across in everyday use from a range of genres (advertisements, newspapers, letters from school, bills, cereal packets, junk mail, and family photograph albums) to work on as a group. Students were to identify to whom the producer was primarily addressing the text, who produced it, why it was interesting, and what message the producer was trying to get across, so that students could see that all writing was created for a particular purpose. Such decoding challenged the participants' assumptions that only one form of writing existed and helped them to see that the writing that they created could vary in form too. Student-led investigations, which involved taking Polaroid photographs of a range of public writing including graffiti, public notices, shop signs, and posters and then coming together to decode these images, enabled discussion to take place about the concerns in the community and the messages that others presented to them. Both these approaches enabled the participants to see the ways in which literacy is constructed in different contexts and for different purposes and led to lively discussions. Two examples were the prevalence of racism in the community as revealed through graffiti on the walls of the houses and the assumption by manufacturers of breakfast cereals of particular family lifestyles, including the presence of two parents in the home.

Sometimes students used the materials that they produced to create a group poem around the discussion's theme; thus, individual contributions led to a collective, cooperative outcome. On other occasions the theme generated letters of complaint to the appropriate authorities; for example, students wrote the authorities to ask for the removal of racist graffiti. The project's general approach was to link reading with writing and talking, bringing these three important facets of literacy together into a seamless web. Project staff regarded oral language as important especially in relation to rhymes, storytelling, and word games, highlighting the importance of using the language of the home and community in other contexts including the school.

Another important aspect of the project was the use of authentic assessment situated in real-life contexts, which project staff did *with* rather than *to* participants. Staff assessed participants' progress according to their ability to make changes in their practices and take action rather than their ability to pass standardized tests. This process-oriented focus involved students developing portfolios of examples of their literacy work as evidence of their learning. Portfolios included the titles of books that they read with their children and copies of stories that they had created about their family life. Other examples were copies of letters they had written to friends and families; diaries; examples of reading and writing done in church, at neighborhood meetings, or at work; and photographs of writing that had interested them. This type of assessment helped the participants to reflect both on what and how they learned and gave them opportunities to test their newly acquired skills. Participants also brought the portfolio to the group for a show-and-tell session, sometimes inviting the children. This approach to assessment enabled those involved to assess the extent to which participants had been able to change their literacy practices. Moreover, it allowed staff and participants to record changes in relationships, particularly with their children and the school. This was a very different approach from the way in which educators normally assess people's learning, using standardized outcome-based methods, and was empowering to both learners and tutors. It enabled learners to take responsibility for their own learning and have an equal say in the direction that it should take. And it provided tutors feedback on the program design, content, and delivery, as well as on the strengths and weaknesses of their approaches.

By taking a problematizing approach to speaking, reading, and writing practices, the project enabled participants to see that there are a variety of literacies rather than just the one that their children's school uses. This in turn helped to challenge the deficit views of the home and community culture that parents had internalized. As they gained confidence in their literacy practices, they were able to interact more equally with the school's staff, becoming involved more directly in their children's education. This required teachers to develop a greater understanding of what parents needed to know about school practices, something that the family literacy project and school staff achieved through joint training sessions. The project also built confidence by helping parents be in a better position to know what to ask the school about their children's progress that took account of the local community culture. For example, using the language (Scots) spoken in the community showed that it was not regarded as slang or otherwise inferior to English. Thus everyday language can become accepted as a language of learning and an educational resource rather than a cultural embarrassment. Parents learned by sharing and valuing experiences as well as by considering suggestions and ideas that the tutor introduced. So the project subtly aided the process of generating new knowledge based on the local culture and context by making the parents' implicit pedagogical activities explicit.

Emphasizing Strengths

This family literacy project made a useful contribution to shifting the definition of the literacy problem. The project curriculum involved the recognition that some people are at a disadvantage because of the ways in which dominant institutions use a particular literacy. "The culture children learn as they grow up is, in fact, 'ways of taking' meaning from the environment around them" (Heath, 1983, p. 49) and not a natural way of behaving. We need to make visible the social practices of the school and other institutions, as well as the language and literacy they reinforce, to show that they represent a selection from a wider range of possibilities—none of which is neutral. These practices then become a critical resource for learning and literacy. An important issue here was the use of Scots for everyday language and literacy. (Scots is a sister language of English that developed differently during the periods of Scottish independence, essentially reflecting greater influences from French and Scandinavian languages.) As the Scottish Consultative Council on the Curriculum (1996, p. 15) has pointed out, because Scots is the language of the home for many people, it provides speakers with their first awareness of themselves and their relationships. Use of the language also helps people to "establish their own sense of values, and [is] closely involved in the development of thinking skills, and those related, equally important, worlds of feeling and social consciousness" (p. 15). Therefore, neglecting the Scots language has unwelcome social and personal consequences.

One important unwelcome consequence that people easily internalize is that the language of their homes and communities is of value only within a very limited range of social contexts. Addison (2001, p. 156) investigated this, asking adult literacy students, "Dae ye speak Scots or slang?" (Do you speak Scots or slang?) Nearly 70 percent of the students responded "I speak slang." Addison points out, "if a community's means of communication and self expression are perceived by themselves to be inferior how then does that reflect on their self-image and confidence"?

When the language and literacy that learners use in the home and community is unacknowledged or actively suppressed, then people find it difficult to say what is important to them in ways that are meaningful. People become voiceless when others do not allow them to speak or allow them to say only what others have said, so they eventually learn how to silence themselves. As long as people remain voiceless, with others interpreting their lived experience, the process renders their own meanings illegitimate and disqualifies them. Giroux (1992, p. 170) has argued that people need to be able "to reclaim their own memories, stories and histories as part of an on-going collective struggle to challenge those power structures that attempt to silence them."

Conclusion

What counts as important knowledge in relation to literacy, access to information, and effective communication skills must come under consideration as part of the way that we systematically reproduce the inequalities of class power. If democracy is to become a way of life, political representatives, public institutions and services, those who work for them (for example, doctors, teachers, welfare workers), and community organizations and groups all have to be accountable to the people they represent or work for. Literacy education should therefore contribute toward enabling people to interrogate others' claims and activities on their behalf and in turn encourage them to develop the skill, analysis, and confidence to make their own voices heard (Crowther and Tett, 2001). Education should also help people to engage in a wide range of political roles and social relationships that occur outside both the workplace and the marketplace. As Halsey (1961, p. v) put it, "the primary concern of [education] should not be with the living that [the students] will earn but with the life they will lead."

Lifelong learning and the opportunities it represents can become a unifying force, not only between providers but also between different interest groups, in ways that ensure that this process challenges oppression and exclusion. This will involve nurturing an education and training system whose function is not to reflect and reproduce existing classed inequalities in society but rather to prioritize provision for those whose earlier educational and socioeconomic disadvantage would give them a first claim in a genuinely lifelong learning system. Educators can then act as an emancipatory force for change, especially if they start "[f]rom the problems, experiences and social position of excluded majorities, from the position of the working people, women and black people. It means working up these lived experiences and insights until they fashion a real alternative" (Johnson, 1988, p. 813). Within this paradigm people's classed and gendered experiences would be a learning resource for them to use, rather than a deficiency for them to rectify.

Knowledge and learning should be something to use, test, question, and produce rather than something to accumulate and assess through qualifications that signify possession of it. Communities in civic society are often seen as needing knowledge that others possess. However, rather than dichotomizing the act of acquiring already existing knowledge from the activity of producing new knowledge, if we see that these two aspects of knowledge are dialectical, then we can transform these relations (see Martin, 2001).

From this perspective learning is essentially about making knowledge that makes sense of the world and helps people to act on it collectively in order to change it for the better. The curriculum always represents selections from a culture (Williams, 1961), so knowledge is never neutral or value-free; what counts as worth knowing reflects those particular class and political interests that have the power to make it count. Change in civil society toward greater equity will involve a radical rethinking of what counts as knowledge and understanding. Knowledge from this position would be actively constructed in the creative encounter between the teacher's expertise and the students' experience, with each role conferring a distinctive kind of authority (see Martin, 2001). Educators have an important role in making sure that they not reduce the complexity of the intellectual, emotional, practical, pleasurable, and political possibilities of learning to the apparent simplicity of targets, standards, and skills (see Thompson, 2001). Finding a voice to do this can happen through being part of a social, mutually supportive group that is engaged in learning. Such learning is both a political and educational activity because it opens up spaces for the public discussion of the issues that concern people.

An emphasis on whose experiences count and how we should interpret and understand them helps us to challenge the so-called common sense of everyday assumptions about experience and their relationship to knowledge production. This allows the making of new claims for the legitimacy of reflexive experience leading to really useful knowledge for those who are involved in generating it. In questioning the discourses that frame the ways of thinking, problems, and practices that society regards as legitimate, people can begin to open up new ways of reflexively thinking about the social construction of their experiences. When people create their own knowledge and know that others hear their voices, this throws into question narrow definitions of what some think to be educated knowledge and who it is that makes it. In this way people can interrogate the experiences and stories that society has excluded and the mystification that so-called expert knowledge has caused as a way of articulating views that come from below rather than above. A popular curriculum that addresses ordinary people's concerns and actively draws on their experience as a resource for educational work in communities increases the possibilities of developing knowledge that is useful to those who generate it.

References

Addison, A. "Using Scots Literacy in Family Literacy Work." In J. Crowther, M. Hamilton, and L. Tett (eds.), *Powerful Literacies*. Leicester, England: National Institute of Adult Continuing Education, 2001.

Archer, L., Hutchings, M., and Ross, A. *Higher Education and Social Class*. London: Routledge Falmer, 2003.

Barton, D., and Hamilton, M. *Local Literacies*. London: Routledge, 1998.

Commission of the European Communities. *A Memorandum on Lifelong Learning*. Brussels: Directorate General for Education, Training and Youth, 2000.

Crowther, J. "Participation in Adult and Community Education: A Discourse of Diminishing Returns." *International Journal of Lifelong Education*, 2000, 19(6), 479–492.

Crowther, J., and Tett, L. "Democracy as a Way of Life. Literacy for Citizenship." In J. Crowther, M. Hamilton, and L. Tett (eds.), *Powerful Literacies*. Leicester, England: National Institute of Adult Continuing Education, 2001.

Department for Education and Employment. *The Learning Age: A Renaissance for a New Britain*. London: Stationery Office, 1998.

Giroux, H. *Border Crossings: Cultural Workers and the Politics of Education*. London: Routledge, 1992.

Halsey, A. H. *Education, Economy and Society*. New York: Free Press, 1961.

Heath, S. B. *Ways with Words: Language, Life and Work in Communities and Classrooms*. Cambridge, England: Cambridge University Press, 1983.

Johnson, R. "Really Useful Knowledge, 1790–1850." In T. Lovett (ed.), *Radical Approaches to Adult Education: A Reader*. London: Routledge, 1988.

Martin, I. "Reconstituting the Agora: Towards an Alternative Politics of Lifelong Learning." *Concept*, 2001, 11(1), 4–8.

McGivney, V. *Education's for Other People*. Leicester, England: National Institute of Adult Continuing Education, 1990.

Sargant, N., and others. *The Learning Divide*. Leicester, England: National Institute of Adult Continuing Education, 1997.

Scottish Consultative Council on the Curriculum. *The Kist: Teacher's Handbook*. Glasgow: Nelson Blackie, 1996.

Taylor, D., and Dorsey-Gaines, C. *Growing Up Literate: Learning from Inner-City Families*. Portsmouth, N.H.: Heinemann, 1988.

Tett, L., and Crowther, J. "Families at a Disadvantage: Class, Culture and Literacies." *British Educational Research Journal*, 1998, 24(4), 449–460.

Thompson, J. *Re-rooting Lifelong Learning*. Leicester, England: National Institute of Adult Continuing Education, 2001.

Wallace, C. "Critical Language Awareness in the EFL Classroom." In N. Fairclough (ed.), *Critical Language Awareness*. White Plains, N.Y.: Longman, 1992.

Williams, R. *Resources for a Journey of Hope*. Harmondsworth, England: Penguin, 1961.

LYN TETT is professor of community education and lifelong learning at the University of Edinburgh, Scotland. Her research focuses on the structural and attitudinal barriers that prevent participation in postcompulsory education.

4

Asserting that the working class has a distinctive learning style, this chapter argues for a supportive, challenging, and class-conscious pedagogy.

Educational Institutions: Supporting Working-Class Learning

Griff Foley

There are two barriers to useful discussion of social class in adult education. First, most scholarship on class and education is about schools. This scholarship, and especially its highly developed ethnographic strand, illuminates adult education practice (see Nesbit, Leach, and Foley, 2004). But to understand properly the dynamics of class in adult education, we need to develop a separate body of research. The second barrier is the widespread denial in our culture of the importance or even the existence of class. The ideological roots and social function of this denial are transparent. If class has disappeared, you are not going to look for it; nor will you need to study it.

The denial of class is so pervasive that I will begin by affirming its existence, in society and in education. The Oxford English Dictionary (OED) provides a leading definition of *class* as "a number of individuals (persons or things) possessing common attributes, and grouped together"; that is, a group of people with something in common. Add *social* to this, and you get "rank, order of society (higher, upper, middle, lower, working; the classes, the rich or educated, opp. the masses)."

So there we have it, from a British establishment institution, the OED. Education and class are connected, and the rich or educated are the upper classes. But let's press on with defining our terms. An *institution* is "an organization for promotion of some public object"—in our case to *educate* people, to "give [them] intellectual and moral training." The Latin root of *educate* is *educare,* whose sense is captured in the rarely used English word *educe:* "to bring out, develop, from latent or potential existence." These definitions express both the promise of our educational institutions (to develop learners, intellectually and morally, for the common good) and their inadequacy (they favor the wealthy and powerful).

New Directions for Adult and Continuing Education, no. 106, Summer 2005 © Wiley Periodicals, Inc.   37

Social class has two qualities. It is a structural reality, arising from people's relationship to the means of production and to political power. Some people own businesses; others sell their labor. Some people wield significant political power; most of us don't. Objectively, there is a working class whose labor produces society's wealth and a class of owners and rulers who exploit workers' labor.

More importantly for our purposes, class is a process, a relationship. As the English historian Thompson (1968) said, class is something that happens in human relationships. Class develops in particular situations over time. It is collective and oppositional. Class happens, Thompson shows in his magisterial history of the formation of the English working class, when through common experience some people articulate a common interest against the interests of others. This expression of a common interest is class consciousness, he writes, which comes to be embodied in traditions, value systems, ideas, and institutions.

But class consciousness and class struggle are not automatic or inevitable. In early essays ("The German Ideology," "Eighteenth Brumaire of Louis Bonaparte"), Marx (cited in Williams, 1976, pp. 67–69) argued that "separate individuals form a class only insofar as they have to carry on a common battle with another class, otherwise they are on hostile terms with each other as competitors." Whatever the objective relationship of a class to the means of production, Marx argued, class becomes politically meaningful only if its members see themselves as being "in hostile opposition" to another class and organize to further their interests. I will argue in this chapter that powerful forces in contemporary society undermine working-class consciousness and organization. But I will also maintain that the continued existence of working-class culture—distinctive values, meanings, institutions, tastes, and lifestyles—provides leverage for furthering the educational interests of the class.

Williams, who came from the Welsh working class, was a grammar school scholarship student, an adult educator, and a Cambridge professor who pioneered cultural studies. He lived and theorized class. In an early essay, Williams (1989, pp. 3–4) writes movingly of the culture he came from, part agricultural, part industrial, fully working class, his grandfather a farm laborer, his father a railway signal man: "To grow up in that family was to see the shaping of minds: the learning of new skills, the shifting of relationships, the emergence of different language and ideas. . . . Learning was ordinary; we learned where we could." When he went to Oxford as a student, culture and learning were not exotic or alienating. What was different was being spared from work to study. This was a privilege that he realized others had won by the collective effort of his people.

What oppressed Williams at university was what he called the culture of the tea shop, the self-conscious cultivation of those who insist that "culture is their trivial differences of behavior, their trivial variations of speech habit" (1989, p. 5). Many of us have encountered this mindless, infuriating superiority, which defines *culture* as arts and learning, the latter being a particular sort of university education. Today few adult educators would subscribe to such a narrow definition of culture and learning. But few too, I think, would have much of an understanding of the broader conception of culture and learning that Williams lived and wrote about.

For culture and learning infuse our lives, and in educational institutions different conceptions of them meet and often clash. This is most obvious in ethnographies of schooling, like Willis's classic study (1977) of English working-class boys resisting what they saw as the effete education the state offered them through their middle-class teachers. More often the culture clash is an unnoticed suppression of subordinate cultures (for an excellent case study of this process in adult education, see Gowen, 1992). Educators have to deal with class as process, as relationship. They are often ill prepared to do this because those in educational institutions and in the wider culture deny class.

The suppression of class in educational institutions reflects its suppression in the wider culture. U.S. mass culture spreads across the world, penetrating even would-be closed societies such as China and Iran, dissolving categories like class that might help us to understand the social forces that shape our world. Yet popular culture also speaks openly of class. Recently a television documentary on Margaret Thatcher showed class struggle at its rawest—police wielding batons as they charged demonstrators, Thatcher and her ministers articulating their contempt for the lower orders. Two days later we saw the film of Evelyn Waugh's novel *Vile Bodies,* which charted the decline into decadence of the aristocracy in 1930s England. Between these two films we saw another film *(Under the Tuscan Sun),* which despite being burdened by a clichéd script and mannered acting, had class at is core—in this case affluent middle-class women searching for meaning.

The trick is, of course, to recognize class when you see it. Increasingly, people cannot, because so much in the culture stops them seeing. The bulk of mass media culture is spectacle, cheap sentiment, sensation, impression management, and stimulated prejudice. We are, of course, not supposed to say this—it sounds elitist, and besides, postmodernism tells us that everything is relative and that we can be playful about it. Postmodernism of course, reflects and feeds the problem by preaching this pap and by ridiculing categories like social class that might help us to understand what mass culture is teaching us and then help us to do something about it.

Social Class and Adult Education

In his study of Canadian workers learning computing, Sawchuk (2003) identifies a distinctive working-class learning style that operates independently of formal training and centers around informal workplace and community networks. This learning style is collective, mutual, and solidaristic. People exchange knowledge and skills, hardware and software. People use each other's differences, which become group resources. And so they develop an expanding learning network: a powerful working-class resource that stands opposed to the trajectory of dominant forms of workplace and institutionalized education that individualize and commodify learning.

Although most research on education and class focuses on how working-class people are excluded and help to exclude themselves from formal education (for example, Rist, 1970; Willis, 1977), Sawchuk's research (2003) shows that working-class adults bring rich cultural resources to their learning. Educational institutions can and sometimes do tap into these resources. Probably the best-studied example of this in the United States is the Highlander Education and Research Center in Tennessee. Here Myles Horton and his colleagues taught working-class people to analyze their experiences critically (Horton and Freire, 1990; Jacobs, 2003). The Highlander pedagogy was conversational yet challenging: it was based on the participants' needs, interests, and principally working-class culture. Other useful accounts of U.S. adult educators working with working-class learning styles include Altenbaugh's description (1990) of the American labor colleges of the 1920s and 1930s and the once extensive but now all-but-forgotten Jefferson School of Social Science, which flourished in New York City during the 1940s and early 1950s (Gettleman, 2002). There have also been several institutional attempts to engage working-class learners in the United Kingdom. For example, Northern College continues to be dedicated to providing high-quality learning experiences for adults whose opportunities for education and training have been limited (Ball and Hampton, 2004). Other examples include Newman's reflections (1993) on trade union education, Head's analyses (1978) of community-based education with London working-class people, and Thompson's discussion (1983) of working-class women's education.

I was reminded of all this recently when I interviewed an old friend, Bob Richardson. I asked him to reflect on his diverse experiences in adult education, as student and teacher. Bob, age sixty-two, was a printer who in his forties became an occupational health and safety (OHS) educator. He ran health and safety training programs at a public utility for many years, where his students ranged from "navvies" (unskilled laborers) to managers. He did a printing apprenticeship in his youth, received a university OHS diploma in his forties, and in his early fifties completed a graduate diploma in adult education at University of Technology, Sydney (UTS). Bob, a lifelong union activist, has also done a lot of trade union education, as student, teacher, and program developer. He still does contract OHS training.

I interviewed Bob because I knew his responses would be interesting and critical. Although I had asked him to consider all his adult education experiences, he spoke mainly about his learning at UTS. Ten years after completing the UTS diploma, Bob said it had been invaluable, giving him a chance to position himself, to assess himself against others. Its focus on reflection enabled him "to plot where I was, who I was. Without it, I wouldn't have achieved what I achieved" in OHS education. For Bob facilitation was a revolutionary concept: "I never thought of myself as being not just a teacher but a facilitator of other people's learning." The course reading also opened him up: "I would never have discovered these people by myself: Freire and others." The program made metaphor and analogy explicit, as well as empathy, self-directed learning, and nonverbal communication: "I'd been using them without knowing that's what I was doing. And I didn't have a reading list."

Bob was comfortable at UTS. "The key to it all was the quality of the people who devise and deliver the education and the way they organized themselves. I'd seen academics before, and they were alien." He had received his OHS diploma at another university in a working-class city. The education had been "extremely formal," the university "very hierarchical." The other students "were not open. They were there to get a degree; they weren't going to share knowledge." The staff didn't counter this, and in this they were "so unlike the UTS people. . . . They did their teaching; there was a barrier. You didn't develop any real relationship with them." The UTS staff were different; they were "people who shared your politics" and taught critical analysis. They taught students to look at what they were doing in their work and why. "I was very lucky," said Bob, then demonstrated how he'd applied his learning.

"I was a corporate trainer, a change agent, overcoming resistance, explaining management's rationale for change, putting the onus for workplace safety onto workers—'It's your fault if you get injured.' So I was supposedly a representative of management. But I wasn't. I developed ways of dealing with assumptions opposite to mine. Critical analysis helped. Adult education is about this: critical analysis of data, any data. It justified my right to criticize the system that paid our wages." Bob rejected the blame-the-worker approach to OHS, telling management that blaming workers for their supposed carelessness with safety was an ineffective way of getting behavioral change. "To change adults," he told them, "you have to give them information which is relevant to their experiences and needs, packaging and unpackaging information until it accorded with the listener"—another thing he said he'd learned about at UTS. I asked Bob what was distinctive about the union education he'd experienced. Unionists, he said, constantly interrupt and challenge you. "'You're wrong, mate,' they'll say, 'but go on.' They assess you on the spot; you have to get around that. That's not a bad thing. UTS showed me its value, so I could use it, not be thrown by it."

From Bob Richardson's account, a pedagogy that respects, builds on, and extends students' experience is the key to making formal education meaningful and useful to working-class adults. Other adult students confirm this. Paul McTigue, a public-sector manager and union organizer who also studied adult education at UTS, spoke of the importance of teachers "validating and valuing" the life experience of adult students. "All of a sudden people are being told their life experience is valuable, and there are things they can learn from it. It's not as if you're an empty vessel to be filled up." To be seen as a "source of knowledge, and important knowledge at that" is often a new experience for adult students.

Over time Paul undertook three UTS adult education programs: associate diploma, bachelor's, and master's. At the outset of each stage, the thought of doing something new filled him with self-doubt. But his teachers quickly dispelled these feelings. "Very quickly I got a sense that the issues and opinions I was grappling with were valid, staff saying these are the things you need to think and write about. These became the meat and potatoes of my study. It wasn't just theory. Your reading and writing all of a sudden has a purpose." Interaction and discussion with other students, many of whom had different social background and work roles from Paul's, reinforced this. There was "a surprising amount of common ground" and "an incredible amount of knowledge in any group" of students.

The UTS educational process, Paul found, was very different from workplace training and learning, which "starts from the employer's idea of where you need to go, not where you're at. . . . Class runs all through this, people undervaluing themselves," with workers' self-doubt shaped by earlier school experience and everyday workplace experience. The discouragement of alternative opinions and ideas in the workplace, this "truly negative learning," according to Paul, has the opposite effect to a pedagogy that validates learners' experience. Workplace pedagogy locks workers into a reluctant acquiescence in existing workplace relations.

As these accounts show, when workers return to study, they need to encounter a pedagogy that is both validating and challenging. In my experience this latter quality—the necessary challenge of education—is one that adult educators who are eager to make their students feel accepted and valued often neglect. The result, as an indigenous Australian adult educator once pointed out (McDaniel and Flowers, 2000, p. 259), is a "quality-compromised" education. I was recently reminded of how important it is to challenge and extend students. A group of adult technical college students was helping our local beach revegetation project by building a dune fence. Afterward I interviewed one of the students. Toni Davies left school at age sixteen, enrolled in a shorthand and typing course that she left before completing to work as a legal secretary, a vocation she followed for thirty-seven years. Two years after retiring, she enrolled in a land conservation and management course, because she'd "always loved plants and gardening and the outdoors." As most adult students do, Toni emphasized the importance of "respect and camaraderie" between teachers and students. But as she talked, it became clear that successful adult study is also a manageable challenge. The intensive, modular nature of her course initially took Toni and other students aback. "I'm no dummy, I'm no slouch," she said. But "you'd just be coming to grips with one module, and you'd have to move on to another. You could lose track of which assignment needed to be done when." The lack of a logical subject sequence exacerbated the problem. The continual assessment of learning, in almost every lesson, was also a challenge. Asked what got her through this, she replied, "My personal character. Once I'm committed, there's no turning back. I'm determined and stubborn and have faith in myself. There's also a lot of self-discipline involved—setting aside the time to study, fitting it in."

A successful adult pedagogy is both supportive and challenging of students. For working-class adults, there is a third essential characteristic: class consciousness. This, of course, is the hardest one for many adult educators to understand, because their own experience and education generally denies the importance or even existence of social class. Working-class students too initially veer away from social class. Toward the end of our conversation, when I mentioned social class, Toni said, "Personally I object to the term. I don't support any class system; they should be eradicated. But most of my friends are left-leaning and are proud to be called working class. I'm working class myself, going back four, probably five generations, right back to Scottish miners. No matter how educated I became, I'd still be a working-class person."

Class consciousness is just below the surface, and much of what happens in educational institutions keeps it there, unexpressed. As we have seen, class infused Paul and Bob's descriptions of their educational experiences. Both are strong unionists, who like Toni were raised working class. Both Bob and Paul's fathers were factory workers. Paul's mother returned to work in her forties and quickly became a union delegate, then a full-time union organizer. Both his parents were active Labor Party members. All three families valued education. Paul's mother's Irish family had a tradition of vocational education, sons following fathers into apprenticeships in the Irish railways. Paul's father taught his three children to read before they started school. His parents and his teachers emphasized the importance of education as "the way ahead to a better life, the entry to a wider world." In his own university professional education, Paul was introduced to Williams, whose essay "Culture Is Ordinary" (in his book *Resources of Hope*, 1989) reinforced Paul's belief that "the vast majority of important creative expression—culture—comes from the so-called lower classes. . . . There's nothing ordinary about the 'ordinary people.'" Williams's autobiographical novel, *Border Country* (1964), struck Paul as "a really loving homage by Williams—a Cambridge don—to his father, family, class, and values—community, people before profit, simplicity, education—and as the way ahead." The insights he encountered at university accorded with and fed Paul's workplace learning, helping him to do his difficult work of furthering workers' interests in a hostile environment. (For Paul's accounts of this work, see Forrester and McTigue, 2004; Foley, 2001.)

Powerful material and cultural forces in contemporary society undermine working-class consciousness and organization. But the continued existence of working-class culture—distinctive values, meanings, institutions, tastes, and lifestyles—provide a basis for furthering workers' educational interests. Sawchuk's study (2003) demonstrates this, as does the way Bob Richardson, Paul McTigue, and Toni Davies talk about their learning and teaching. Adult educators who wish to support working-class learning need to learn to recognize and work with working-class culture and to establish links with working-class institutions (for a good example of the latter, see Forrester and McTigue, 2004).

References

Altenbaugh, R. J. *Education for Struggle: American Labor Colleges of the 1920s and 1930s.* Philadelphia: Temple University Press, 1990.

Ball, M., and Hampton, W. (eds.). *The Northern College: 25 Years of Adult Learning.* Leicester, England: National Institute of Adult Continuing Education, 2004.

Foley, G. *Strategic Learning: Understanding and Facilitating Workplace Change.* Sydney: UTS Centre for Popular Education, 2001.

Forrester, K., and McTigue, P. "Workplace Learning." In G. Foley (ed.), *Dimensions of Adult Learning: Adult Education and Training in a Global Era.* Sydney and London: Allen & Unwin/Open University Press, 2004.

Gettleman, M. E. "'No Varsity Teams': New York's Jefferson School of Social Science, 1943–1956." *Science & Society,* 2002, 66(3), 336–359.

Gowen, S. *The Politics of Workplace Literacy.* New York: Teachers College Press, 1992.

Head, D. *There's No Politics Here.* London: City Lit, 1978.

Horton, M., and Freire, P. *We Make the Road by Walking: Conversations on Education and Social Change.* Philadelphia: Temple University Press, 1990.

Jacobs, D. (ed.). *The Myles Horton Reader: Education for Social Change.* Knoxville: University of Tennessee Press, 2003.

McDaniel, M., and Flowers, R. "Adult Education and Indigenous Australians." In G. Foley (ed.), *Understanding Adult Education and Training.* (2nd ed.) St. Leonards, Australia: Allen & Unwin, 2000.

Nesbit, T., Leach, L., and Foley G. "Teaching Adults." In G. Foley (ed.), *Dimensions of Adult Learning: Adult Education and Training in a Global Era.* Sydney and London: Allen & Unwin/Open University Press, 2004.

Newman, M. *The Third Contract: Theory and Practice in Trade Union Training.* Sydney: Stewart Victor Publishing, 1993.

Rist, R. "Student Social Class and Teacher Expectations." *Harvard Educational Review,* 1970, 40(3), 411–451.

Sawchuk, P. H. *Adult Learning and Technology in Working-Class Life.* New York: Cambridge University Press, 2003.

Thompson, E. P. *The Making of the English Working Class.* Harmondsworth, England: Penguin, 1968.

Thompson, J. *Learning Liberation: Women's Response to Men's Education.* London: Croom Helm, 1983.

Williams, R. *Border Country.* Harmondsworth, England: Penguin, 1964.

Williams, R. *Keywords: A Vocabulary of Culture and Society.* London: Flamingo, 1976.

Williams, R. *Resources of Hope: Culture, Democracy, Socialism.* London: Verso, 1989.

Willis, P. *Learning to Labour: How Working-Class Kids Get Working-Class Jobs.* Farnborough, England: Saxon House, 1977.

GRIFF FOLEY is a research associate of the Centre for Popular Education, University of Technology, Sydney. He has published on a wide variety of adult education topics; his most recent book is Adult Education and Training in a Global Era *(2004).*

5

This chapter considers how class helps to construct the identity and ultimately the teaching of certain groups of educators, and it explores ways of making class explicit in the teacher education classroom.

Class in the Classroom

Janice Malcolm

> The loss of historical consciousness and critical distance is a major impediment to the development of purposeful practice in the current context in which higher education is rapidly becoming not only the object but also a key instrument of the dominant hegemony.
> —Ian Martin and Mae Shaw (1997, p. 305)

In Britain and elsewhere, the curriculum of adult education and of pedagogic training and education is increasingly subject to central determination and regulation within a policy framework that promotes social inclusion as a means to economic competitiveness and thus to a more cohesive society. But because of the historic class-related divisions within education, the impact of this regulatory incursion is clearly differentiated according to the nature of institutions and their students. For example, free education for adults is largely limited to the development of literacy, numeracy, and English language; and major national campaigns exhort and persuade the undereducated individual to improve these basic skills through a variety of initiatives, including learning at work. The New Deal initiative in Britain targets unemployed people, particularly single parents, individually channeling them into work-related training; it ensures that people see that taking a low-paid job is preferable to living on welfare benefits, and the threat to withdraw those benefits clearly reinforces the message. Initiatives targeting parents living in deprived areas (like this one from Sure Start) aim to support "parents as parents and in their aspirations towards employment"

Author's note: Thanks to Paul Armstrong, teaching collaborator and inspiration over many years.

(Department for Education and Skills and Department for Work and Pensions, 2004), through both childcare and parental education focusing on parenting skills and children's nutrition, education, and development. Initiatives of this kind will be familiar to educators around the world, not just Britain. Their aims are educational in the most instrumental sense: they seek to combat social and economic problems by targeting individuals that society sees as deficient in terms of skills, attitude, or behavior.

For much of the twentieth century, the ostensible justification for a policy of differentiated and stratified educational provision was that children and adults should receive an education suitable to their "aptitudes and abilities" (*Education Act, 1944*); however, it was clearly the case that most people received the (usually limited) education that society deemed appropriate to their class and gender. Class has become obscured over recent years both as a political category and as a basis for educational analysis, in a way that reflects some of the political changes of the last few decades. The increasingly global rise of a taken-for-granted analysis within which individuals and self-interest are the primary locus and explanation of social activity is mirrored in the curricular and pedagogic practices now fundamentally reshaping adult education. Much contemporary pedagogic discourse has abandoned class as a collective motivating and explanatory category in favor of individualist characterizations of need, learning, achievement, and so on. At the same time, the bland policy discourses of inclusion and participation, with their focus on promoting and measuring the engagement of excluded groups in educational activities, serve to distract attention from the crucial question of what, why, and how these newly included learners are learning. "The inclusion/exclusion debate defines the problem of poverty and lack of access to social and economic resources as being about the dysfunction of particular groups in those communities. The solution offered in this model is for these people to adjust to a taken-for-granted middle class norm of behavior, such as re-training, to enable integration" (Stuart, 2000, p. 27).

So although class has become to a large extent unspeakable as an analytical category, policy increasingly embeds class and other inequalities not only within educational structures but also in the discourses and practices of teaching, learning, assessment, and accreditation. Thus, class becomes yet more firmly located within the classroom itself.

Class and Pedagogic Learning

In this chapter I draw on my work with a specific group of students: nongraduate teachers and teaching assistants working in further education colleges (the U.K. equivalent of community or two-year colleges) and schools. Many of them will have left school at the earliest opportunity and trained in skilled work or taken on relatively low-skilled jobs that required little training. The nongraduate teachers may have progressed to a fairly high level in a skilled occupation (for example, construction, secretarial work), before coming to work in colleges as vocational teachers without a teaching quali-fication. Some of the women working as teaching assistants in schools have spent long periods at home raising families and have come into educational work—of an unqualified and very low-paid kind—through the process of helping out in their children's schools or doing other voluntary work related to their mothering role. Many are hoping eventually to become school-teachers, though this is a long and difficult path from their starting point.

Both of the occupations represented here are in their different ways of low status and are in the process of professionalizing through higher edu-cation qualifications. Many of the students are from working-class back-grounds, although they may not think of themselves in this way. Both the nongraduate teachers and the teaching assistants are likely to be having their first experience of higher education within our programs of profes-sional adult education, and they are often the first members of their fami-lies to enter a university. The students thus represent a familiar adult education profile, with the added complication that they are also in the process of becoming educators themselves. In this sense they could be prime examples of the problematic relationship between working-class stu-dents and education; these students may be seeking a form of self-realiza-tion through education, but "higher education poses a threat to both authenticity and a coherent sense of selfhood" (Reay, 2001, p. 337) for them. At the same time, it places them in a powerful position as educators of others.

In educational terms what unites these groups is that they have had an experience of education that has led them into relatively low-status, albeit often skilled, work and within which the ability to analyze and think criti-cally has been of very minor importance. Contemporary educators and pol-icymakers might well see them as educational failures in a context in which we now expect 50 percent of those who leave school to go into higher edu-cation. This is not just a British issue; "even in Canada's relatively open class society, universities remain very effective reproducers of class-based cre-dentialed knowledge privileges" (Livingstone, 1997, p. 287).

These students are living examples of the way in which class helps to construct the educational experience of individuals and the way that often impoverished experience in turn constructs their life chances and under-standings. As Mahony and Zmroczek (1997, p. 4) put it, "[class] is more like a foot that carries us forward than a footprint which marks a past presence." Not having generally succeeded in education and consequently working in relatively low-status occupations, the students often attribute their social and economic position to their individual lack of success in education rather than to the factors such as class that have constructed their educational experience. This focus on individual pathology as an explanation for success or failure is a particularly pernicious characteristic of contemporary British educational discourse: "a disturbing number of adults appear to be disinterested (*sic*) in further learning or cannot see its relevance to them. . . . we must find ways of reaching this group, changing their attitudes and overcoming their inertia" (Department for Education and Employment, 2000, p. 1).

"Education for the working class has traditionally been about failure" (Reay, 2001, p. 334), but the causes to which some attribute this failure have undergone a change as class has withered as an explanatory educational and political category. "The growing gap between the rich and poor has become an accepted part of the 'way things are' for many in England, often understood through discourses of individualization which attribute material success or failure to either individual effort, individual talent or a mixture of the two" (p. 335).

The learning and teaching and the social inclusion discourses within which these students carry out their own educational work now perpetuates and reinforces this attribution of failure. Although the personal outcome of their education to date is neither unusual nor surprising in the light of their class backgrounds, these students frequently offer pathological explanations of their own educational underachievement in terms of personal inadequacy or particular attitudes and pressures within their own families or communities. This individualized view of the way things are may in turn inform their pedagogic understandings as they work with their own so-called underachieving or socially excluded learners.

The current policy context in many wealthy countries explicitly uses educational initiatives as an economic and social tool. As McGivney (2001, p. 9) points out, the implementation of "widening participation" policies "has important social as well as economic aims and is a process that is intended to change the behavior and hence the prospects of the socially excluded and disaffected. . . . this enjoins on people . . . a certain sense of moral responsibility to engage in purposeful learning." The curricula and syllabi that our students are required to deliver to their own learners, whether targeted or more mainstream, frequently focus on differentiated and individualized programs of learning and require that learners take increasing responsibility for planning, monitoring, and evaluating their individual learning—and by extension, for their consequent success or failure. Educators are teaching the lesson that educational failure is the learners' fault more carefully and effectively than ever before.

This pedagogic version of the way things are is clearly evident in the curricula and standards that government-sponsored regulatory bodies prescribe for teachers and teaching assistants. In Britain's further education colleges, where the majority of working-class students are enrolled, teachers are now required to undergo an extremely prescriptive training program underpinned by prescribed values and notions of pedagogic professionalism (Further Education National Training Organisation [FENTO], 1999; Malcolm and Zukas, 2000). Teachers are subject to regular managerial rather than developmental observations of teaching and to external quality inspections in which others judge and grade their teaching and the attainment of their students (practices that are not required in universities). The teacher education standards demand that the syllabus cover hundreds of detailed items, of which the following are merely illustrative (FENTO, 1999; emphasis added):

- Assess the experience, capabilities and learning styles of individual learners in relation to the identified learning program
- Agree [sic] learning goals and targets that support individual needs and aspirations within available resources
- Contribute to management information systems and ensure that colleagues are given all necessary information at the correct time and in the agreed organizational format
- Promote the concept that learners have a responsibility for ensuring that their learning is successful
- Explore ways of encouraging learners to work effectively on their own and to take more responsibility for ensuring that their learning is successful
- Use their own experience of learning to inform their approach to teaching

To any critical adult educator considering what teaching is about and how best to do it, these glib prescriptions are crying out for analysis and must inevitably invite the questions: Why? For whose benefit? How? Yet the standards obscure questions of this kind; they take for granted the values and analysis that inform the statements as simply the pedagogic way things are. They leave little space to develop an understanding of learning as a social and cultural practice in which educators and learners enact and perpetuate social relations existing outside the classroom.

Making Class Visible in the Classroom

How can we, as adult educators and teacher educators, ensure that an explicit understanding of the relationship between class and education is available to our students? I would argue that such an understanding is an essential element of teacher education, yet it is absent from the prescribed curriculum. Moreover, the pedagogic assumptions permeating both the curriculum and the culture of educational workplaces constrain the ways in which we can use pedagogy as an aid to understanding. My response to these difficulties is to use every opportunity to engage students in thinking about why the teacher education standards require them to undergo particular educational processes, teach certain syllabi, perform in specific ways. A few brief examples of how to pose this question will suffice here; clearly, different learning settings will generate different and possibly more imaginative responses to the problem.

One way of making class explicit in the classroom is to insist that students study both the history of education and their own educational history. The history of education was for many years an integral part of teacher education programs; this may well still be the case in some countries, but in Britain it has all but disappeared from the prescribed teacher education curriculum. But it is very difficult to grasp why the education system and its cultural practices look the way they do, without knowing how they were shaped and constructed from a historical perspective. The struggles for working-class education in the nineteenth century, the lengthy debates over whether and how to educate women, the unpleasant realities of early twentieth-century attitudes to the education of the so-called mentally unfit, the gradual dawning of awareness that educators were subjecting immigrant children and adults to educational apartheid—knowledge of these issues is an essential contribution to any explanation of contemporary educational structures and practices. It is immensely helpful for students to be able to trace the development of educational discourses over time and to explore the idea that "such unexamined discursive constructs as . . . 'inner-city disadvantage' are coded class and racialized signifiers of the assumed deficiencies that working-class students bring with them" (Mac an Ghaill, 1996, p. 170).

Asking students to consider their own educational history provides a further opportunity for them to locate themselves as social and historical actors. Once they have understood the historical context of educational practices, students find it less easy to attribute their lack of educational success to individual or family pathology. This in turn helps them to see their own students as culturally and historically located and to challenge assumptions about individual dysfunction or disaffection. Most important, this process brings class and other aspects of the social world into the classroom—from which discourses of individualism and, most recently, so-called personalized learning have excluded them (Department for Education and Skills [DES], 2004).

Students are often resistant to the inclusion of historical study in a teacher education program. They may see it as quite irrelevant to the daily realities of teaching and the demands of the workplace; some students demand that we just show them how to teach. And yet this view is in itself an example of how the attitudes and pedagogic identities of teachers and teaching assistants are constructed through workplace practices and popular readings of education policy. Such policy encourages them to see themselves as technicians, pedagogic operatives who simply carry out technical procedures within a framework that someone else has prescribed; challenging this antiprofessional version of pedagogic identity can be very difficult in the face of their daily experience of educational practice. Appeals to professionalism are problematic for adult educators who may see the idea as elitist and, in effect, a manifestation of conventional self-interest on the part of middle-class occupational groups. However, promoting an idea of professionalism as "reclaiming teaching" (Smyth, 1995, p. 4), as resistance, challenge, and the power to say no, can be both energizing and antielitist. The condition that teacher education meet professional requirements (FENTO, 1999) provides the necessary curricular space within which students can begin to challenge the current received educational wisdom and develop what Williams (1983, p. 243) called the "resources for a journey of hope."

The development of a historical perspective also helps to lay bare the myth of education as a necessary handmaiden to what is now euphemistically called economic competitiveness. Many of these teacher-students wrestle on a daily basis with the irreconcilable contradiction between being student-centered—focusing on the needs of the individual student—and meeting the requirements of education policy, which explicitly places "employers in the driving seat, with colleges and training providers who know how to help business and respond to their needs" (DES, 2004, p. 8). The idea that the purpose of education—and especially adult education— is and should be primarily to meet the needs of the capitalist economy for labor at appropriate skill levels has become firmly rooted in the education system's culture and practices. This is the first chance that many students have to explore alternative ideas on the purpose of education or its relationship to the economy. It is neither necessary nor particularly practical to expect students to embark on a detailed theoretical analysis of education as a process for the generation of surplus value (Rikowski, 2001), but it is certainly possible to encourage them to step back from everyday educational discourses and practices to consider whose interests they serve.

For example, we can use as a starting point a statement such as this: "The skills of our people are a vital national asset. Skills help businesses achieve the productivity, innovation and profitability needed to compete. They help our public services provide the quality and choice that people want. They help individuals raise their employability, and achieve their ambitions for themselves, their families and their communities" (DES, 2003, p. 5). This enables students to unpack the meaning and implications of government policy on adult education and to identify the pedagogic and economic assumptions on which it is built. Teacher-students can interrogate taken-for-granted classroom practices such as individual needs analyses and learning contracts in the light of alternative interpretations of educational purposes, underpinned by historical understandings and the awareness they bring that nothing about educational practices is inevitable.

There is nothing particularly new in making the case for adult educators to consider class as a major aspect of educational purposes and practices—although this may be a more or less familiar form of analysis depending on one's cultural context. I was surprised to hear a colleague from the United States, at an Adult Education Research Conference symposium on this topic in 2004, state that some students would be reluctant to admit to working-class origins. Specific political traditions may present different challenges, particularly in contexts that generally reject class as a way of thinking about the world. However, it does seem necessary to restate the importance of hanging on to class as a category in the face of growing centralization and curricular prescription in teacher education at all levels. As educators, we are, as the opening quotation from Martin and Shaw (1997,

p. 305) states, a "key instrument" in either perpetuating or challenging particular forms of dominance; we can choose which side to be on.

References

Department for Education and Employment. *Tackling the Adult Skills Gap: Upskilling Adults and the Role of Workplace Learning.* London: Department for Education and Employment, 2000.
Department for Education and Skills (DES). *Twenty-First Century Skills: Realising Our Potential; Individuals, Employers, Nation.* London: Department for Education and Skills, 2003.
Department for Education and Skills (DES). *Five Year Strategy for Children and Learners.* London: Department for Education and Skills, 2004.
Department for Education and Skills and Department for Work and Pensions. "Sure Start." [http://www.surestart.gov.uk]. Accessed March 4, 2004.
Education Act (7&8 Geo 6 c. 31). London: HMSO, 1944.
Further Education National Training Organisation (FENTO). *Standards for Teaching and Supporting Learning in Further Education in England and Wales.* London: Further Education National Training Organisation, 1999.
Livingstone, D. W. "Working-Class Culture, Adult Education and Informal Learning: Beyond the 'Cultural Capital' Bias to Transformative Community." In P. Armstrong, N. Miller, and M. Zukas (eds.), *Crossing Borders, Breaking Boundaries: Research in the Education of Adults.* London: SCUTREA, 1997.
Mac an Ghaill, M. "Sociology of Education, State Schooling and Social Class: Beyond Criticisms of the New Right Hegemony." *British Journal of Sociology of Education,* 1996, 17(2), 163–176.
Mahony, P., and Zmroczek, C. "Why Class Matters." In C. Zmroczek and P. Mahony (eds.), *Class Matters: "Working Class" Women's Perspectives on Social Class.* London: Taylor and Francis, 1997.
Malcolm, J., and Zukas, M. "Looking-Glass Worlds: Pedagogy in Further and Higher Education." Paper presented at FE Research Network Conference, University of Warwick, England, December 2000.
Martin, I., and Shaw, M. "Sustaining Social Purpose in the Current Policy Context." In P. Armstrong, N. Miller, and M. Zukas (eds.), *Crossing Borders, Breaking Boundaries: Research in the Education of Adults.* London: SCUTREA, 1997.
McGivney, V. *Fixing or Changing the Pattern? Reflections on Widening Adult Participation in Learning.* Leicester, England: National Institute of Adult Continuing Education, 2001.
Reay, D. "Finding or Losing Yourself? Working-Class Relationships to Education." *Journal of Education Policy,* 2001, 16(4), 333–346.
Rikowski, G. "After the Manuscript Broke Off: Thoughts on Marx, Social Class and Education." Paper presented to British Sociological Association Education Study Group, Kings College, London, June 23, 2001.
Smyth, J. (ed.). *Critical Discourses in Teacher Development.* London: Cassell, 1995.
Stuart, M. "Beyond Rhetoric: Reclaiming a Radical Agenda for Active Participation in Higher Education." In J. Thompson (ed.), *Stretching the Academy: The Politics and Practice of Widening Participation in Higher Education.* Leicester, England: National Institute of Adult Continuing Education, 2000.
Williams, R. *Towards 2000.* Harmondsworth, England: Penguin, 1983.

JANICE MALCOLM is a senior lecturer at the University of Kent, England, and worked for many years at the University of Leeds. She is a teacher educator and researches teachers' development of pedagogic identity, both through teacher education and in the workplace.

6

Social movements in South Africa, often organized around class-related issues, provide rich material to illustrate how class, intertwined with other social categories, shapes organizational and educational practices.

Social Movements, Class, and Adult Education

Shirley Walters

Social movements are movements of people in civil society who cohere around issues and identities that they themselves define as significant (Martin, 1999). The following quotation describes a group of poor women in South Africa, a group calling itself People's Dialogue, who are mobilizing around their need for houses. They are part of a social movement of women and men internationally who are collectively struggling for access to land and houses.

Women are singing
Ululating, dancing,
Marching
Carrying placards for their different housing associations,
Wearing T shirts which read—
People's Dialogue for Housing and Shelter
We Want!
Power! Money! Knowledge!

The songs they sing tell of the hardships they endure in the shacks, the threat from fire, rain and the wind from eviction even under a new government.

Now they have started to build houses by saving R2 [two South African rands (equivalent to 35 U.S. cents)] a day.

These women are marching to the mass meeting in Hout Bay settlement, Imizamo Yethu. The atmosphere is electric, there is lots of energy, excitement and anxiety as the different housing savings groups take the courage to say

NEW DIRECTIONS FOR ADULT AND CONTINUING EDUCATION, no. 106, Summer 2005 © Wiley Periodicals, Inc. 53

enough is enough, we are tired of this kind of life, and don't want to die in fires any longer and they say, 'We work with all our hearts to do the good work and do not want to be pitied and we will rebuild our lives as we build our homes'" (Ismail, 2003, p. 94).

The fact that the women from People's Dialogue are poor, they speak IsiXhosa, and they are women shapes very much what they do and how they do it. This chapter will examine how particularly notions of class affect the education in and the learning fostered by social movements. I will begin with a discussion of what social movements are and what adult education and learning means in relation to them. I will then focus in on South African social movements as a "mirror and lens" (Crowther, Martin, and Shaw, 1999, p. 2) in order to draw out key issues. In this era of globalization, South Africa is a microcosm of wider processes at work in other societies. It is a middle-income country that has recently emerged from a protracted liberation struggle; and its reentry into the global economy is heightening the tensions between economic development, equity, and redress. As such, South Africa is both a mirror reflecting these processes and a lens through which to examine them.

What Are Social Movements?

Social movements are voluntary associations of people and organizations within civil society that rise and fall in response to particular social, economic, ideological, and political changes and issues often driven by the state or the market. They are reactive and are sustained by their relationships to the particular issues or circumstances. A common feature of much social-movement activity is its oppositional or alternative nature. Social movements are the lightning rods of society. They can be either conservative reactionary forces or progressive. The focus in this chapter is on the latter.

Welton (quoted in Martin, 1999) identifies three general characteristics of social movements: they articulate a collective identity, which means that their members subscribe to a common cause that the movement expresses collectively; they exist in an antagonistic relation to an opposed group or interest; they have a normative orientation, which means that they embody a mobilizing ethic, moral code, or set of beliefs that reflect shared values and purposes.

Social movements have a long history around the world, for example, within anticolonial struggles, among peasants and workers, the urban poor, black people, and women. Oppressed and exploited people have fought back against their harsh material realities through collective organizing. Many social movements have historically organized around class-related issues. Eyerman and Jamison (1991, p. 62) say that social movements are "at once conditioned by the historical contexts in which they emerge, their particular time and place, and, in turn, affect that context through their cognitive and political praxis." To understand the workings of particular social movements, you therefore have to locate them quite particularly.

Melucci (quoted in Badat, 1999, p. 29) argues that we should see social movements as "action systems operating in a systemic field of possibilities and limits. . . . Social movements are action systems in that they have structures: the unity and continuity of action would not be possible without integration and interdependence of individuals and groups." In many instances a social movement comprises various smaller interdependent organizational structures, working toward a particular social goal. The social movement in turn may well form a coalition with other social movements, in order to create a united front to oppose an issue or promote an idea.

Through participation in social movements, people prepare for change or resistance to it by challenging or confirming the ways in which they think and feel and act politically. Their moral or counterhegemonic work may become the common sense of an era. As Martin (1999, p. 10) states, "in this sense social movements are intrinsically educative both for the participants and for the broader society."

Social-Movement Learning

Eyerman and Jamison (1991) have made a seminal contribution to understanding learning in social movements. They state (p. 14): "Social movements are not merely social dramas; they are the social action from where new knowledge including worldviews, ideologies, religions, and scientific theories originate." Because adult education is integral to social processes and therefore social movements, it is not surprising that it gains in prominence at heightened political or economic moments in response to actions within the state, civil society, or the private sector.

Social-movement learning includes both learning by people who participate in social movements and learning by people outside of social movements through the impact they make (Hall and Clover, 2005). Learning through a movement can occur informally through participation or through intentional educational interventions. The educational and organizational practices intertwine. The cultural, gender, class, and ethnic locations of the individuals or groups involved shape the educational and organizational practices, just as they are shaped by the particular historical conjuncture. Social movements are exceedingly rich learning environments. So in those movements organized around class-related issues such as working conditions, housing, health, and other social services, participants come to realize that collective action and solidarity, as captured in the workers' slogan "an injury to one is an injury to all," is the most effective approach to overcome social and economic hardships.

I turn now to explore what these ideas mean in a specific context through a description of social movements in South Africa, with a particular focus on the ways that social class shapes organizational and educational practices.

Social Movements in South Africa

Over the last hundred years in South Africa, civil society has responded to political, social, cultural, and economic hardships through mobilizing people across social class, ethnicity, gender, and geography into social movements. During the 1970s, 1980s, and early 1990s, the political social movements for democracy were particularly prominent. These movements adopted innovative organizational and educational processes to encourage women and men of all classes and racial categories to participate actively in the movement for change. In 1994 national liberation was achieved. More recently social movements have again formed in response to economic and social hardships in relation to land and privatization of basic services (like water), HIV/AIDS, and violence against women and children; some have strong links to international social movements. Each of the social movements has a different composition of membership depending on its social purposes. Some, for example, are rooted very particularly among the landless and the poor, others among middle-class, working-class, and poor women. The composition of movements shapes profoundly the organizational and educational activities within them. I will draw on a study (Walters, 1989) of self-education within the social movements in the 1980s, which shows this clearly.

The history of resistance in South Africa from the early twentieth century involves a complex interplay between national political organizations and social-movement struggles; Abrahams (1996) provides a succinct description of this. The social-movement struggles have had a significant effect on the development of strategic perspectives of political organizations. When the African National Congress (ANC) was formed in 1912, it reflected an attempt to unite people, who until then had resisted colonialism in scattered and disparate ways, into a national political movement. The development of capitalism in South Africa in the latter half of the nineteenth century had destroyed the traditional precapitalist social formations of the indigenous people. The political, social, and economic institutions that emerged during those early years gave the South African social formation its peculiar racial capitalist character. The early national liberation movement, mainly made up of the ANC, whose leadership came almost entirely from the ranks for the emergent African middle class, had no mass membership and in many ways represented the social and political outlook of that social class. As Abrahams argues, this outlook sharply circumscribed the political strategies and tactics the ANC advocated and employed.

In mass protests women resisted an attempt to extend the notorious pass laws to them, forcing the state to drop the idea temporarily. (Pass laws prescribed who could enter, live, and work in certain areas. The common result was that black men and women had to carry a pass on them at all times or face punishment and imprisonment.) The conservative ANC leadership was forced to respond to social-movement struggles engineered and led by people in communities and in the mines. The Communist Party of South Africa, formed in 1921, provided a very important theoretical input that helped shape the early perspectives of the nascent liberation movement. One of the factors that made class alliances possible was a shared oppression that all black people in South Africa experienced.

In the early 1940s, numerous social movements of the poor emerged in response to people's worsening economic, social, and political positions. The enormously exploitative conditions that oiled the wheels of white capitalism meant that issues such as housing, cost of living, fuel, transport, and clothing all became highly contentious political issues for black people. Numerous grassroots social movements emerged in the urban slums, arising out of local frustrations at appalling conditions. Their emerging leadership was not of the same social class or outlook as that of the existing political organizations. However, they began processes that effectively pushed organizations like the ANC toward the left. Such social movements were defensive responses by the working class and poor to socioeconomic crises. They tended to have short life spans. The ANC began to provide the glue to bond them into a sustainable movement to end white minority rule, a movement that conformed to the three characteristics of social movements that Welton (quoted in Martin, 1999) identified: a collective identity of oppressed people, an antagonistic relationship with the white minority government, and a vision of a nonracial democratic state.

In this early period, the impact of poor and working-class people on the shape and form of the liberation movement was marked. They influenced what the movement took up and how. Evidence of this influence was visible in the 1950s when the ANC changed into a mass-based organization that adopted strikes, boycotts, mass protests, and general civil disobedience as its new weapons. Seeking the destruction of white minority rule necessitated creation of the broadest front of resistance because it affected people across class, social, and racial lines. It thus laid the basis for the potential unity of those social forces and classes. Among the white people were also those prepared to throw in their lot with the oppressed in pursuit of nonracial democracy.

The 1960s was a quiet period because the state had banned political organizations and jailed their leadership. The ANC set itself up in exile and established its military wing. The social movements of the 1970s and 1980s can be traced back to these earlier periods. As Melucci (quoted in Badat, 1999, p. 32) states, it is important to recognize the relationship between the visible and latent dimensions of collective action: during the latency phase, "the potential for resistance or opposition is sewn into the very fabric of daily life. It is located in the molecular experience of the individuals and groups who practice the alternative meanings of everyday life. Within this context, resistance is not expressed in collective forms of conflictual mobilizations. Specific circumstances are necessary for opposition and therefore of mobilizing and making visible this latent potential." Thus, phases of latency, far from being periods of inaction, are crucial to the formation and development of abilities and capacities for mobilization and struggle.

The formation of the United Democratic Front (UDF) in 1983 was a culminating point of the reemergence of popular struggles in the 1970s and responses to the state's restructuring. The UDF comprised thousands of sector organizations nationally. Two of the most significant social-movement formations within the UDF were the trade union movement and community-based residents' associations that formed around specific issues. The independent trade union movement was emphasizing the importance of worker democracy within the unions and the workplace as an essential part of the broader struggle for democracy; this movement did not join the UDF until later. Its participants saw community organizations as unaccountable and were at times critical of middle-class leadership.

Through the collective struggles with community organizations, the differences between the forms and functions of trade unions and other organizations came into focus. The unions initially argued against affiliation to the UDF because they saw the different class composition of the various affiliates as leading to different possibilities for organizational forms and strategies. There were ideological struggles in the unions themselves between those who emphasized organizing in the workplace and those who argued for closer worker-community solidarity. Harsh repression from the state forced closer work among and across organizations.

Besides differences across class and organizational forms, racial differences intersected with class. Within the apartheid hierarchy, the African townships were the most impoverished; and Webster (in Walters, 1989) found that the working class and the poor devised all sorts of strategies to cope with their poverty and oppression. Many people were engaged in informal sector activities such as brewing beer and hawking food, and they fleshed out their inadequate income through small self-help groups like burial societies and credit societies. They were defensive responses. Molefe (quoted in Walters, 1989, p. 120) found that it was more difficult in African areas to establish more structured community organizations: "We see less of a natural drift towards committees or formal styles of organizations." He comments on the lower levels of repression in the Indian and Coloured areas than in African areas. (The racial hierarchy privileged white, then Indian, then Coloured, then black Africans. This meant that residential areas reflected the degree of privilege and deprivation in that order.) Organizations were therefore less vulnerable. The level of repression also forced many Africans to believe that the only viable option was a military one. Thus, the repression aided recruitment for the liberation army rather than for small-scale relatively reformist community struggles. Molefe's third point was that the greater degree of material deprivation created organizational possibilities. There were limited resources for people to draw on. People who had overcome the struggle for survival had more time and inclination to engage in other struggles. These realities played out in the ways that organizations operated. For example, in African townships people were mobilized mainly through mass meetings; in Coloured areas there was more door-to-door organizing. The symbolic and cultural forms that organizations used also varied across ethnic groups. Singing, dancing, and ululating were integral to African-led organizations, as we see in the opening quotation.

Within organizations like the United Women's Organisation, an important affiliate of the UDF, the class and cultural alliances among women were significant. The organization was formed into branches based in geographical areas in Cape Town. Because of the ecology of the apartheid city, this meant that each of the branches adopted a distinctive profile in terms of racial, language, and class differences. The older African women and some Coloured women, who had status from their close involvement with the liberation movement, provided the political leadership. The white middle-class women played a support role, although each branch had the autonomy to shape its own activities. So the participants' biographies influence particular branches' activities. For example, one branch of mainly white women did a popular history project to highlight the devastating effects of the Group Areas Act, while an African branch organized a march to the local shop against hikes in bread prices. The white women, because of their privileged class positions, were able to provide transport and other organizational infrastructure to support organizing in the poor working-class areas.

Learning within the social movements was conscious. Most of the affiliated organizations promoted participatory democratic practices as a way of building members' capacities. Originating in the Black Consciousness Movement was the imperative for black people to gain confidence and capacity to lead. Within the nascent women's movement was the commitment to develop women, particularly black working-class women. In the trade unions was the need to build worker leadership. The emphasis was on collective leadership and learning by doing. However, as Walters (1989) describes in great detail, the participatory democratic practices were shaped by the origins and purposes of the organization, the members' biographies, and members' theoretical understandings of their actions. Those who were most closely allied to the movement in exile had stronger accountability to that; whereas others emphasized the importance of the collective inside the country, township, or organization. The tensions between accountability to the collective within one affiliate and to the broader movements, both inside the country and in exile, were palpable. These often had racial, class, and other historical dimensions.

The influence of ideologies and philosophies from international social movements on the ways of organizing was also apparent. The works of the Italian Marxist Gramsci and Brazilian Freire, among others, were widely read. The radical students, worker, women's, and black movements in North America and Europe were also influential, as were the anticolonial struggles in Africa.

The contemporary social movements in South Africa are influenced by the intense social mobilizing of the earlier years of struggle. There are both continuities and breaks with the past. As Ismail (2003, p. 100) describes the women of the South African Homeless People's Federation, "They sing various hymns, slogans, traditional songs, which they often combine with protest songs from the struggle days, and new protest songs from the Federation. They sing about the hardship of being in shacks that are prone to rain and evictions." What is new is that they have strong relationships internationally as they build "globalization from below" (Marshall, 1997, p. 57). They have, for example, special relations with the National Slum Dwellers Federation in India, and their education has been enriched through exchange programs with them. The people's development strategies resonate with working-class and poor women's pedagogy in other parts of the world (Walters and Manicom, 1996; Foley, 1999). Although the hegemony of the neoliberal global economy ensures that the struggles continue for poor and working-class women and men in South Africa, they are reacting in new and creative ways.

In Closing

Social movements are privileged locations for the creation of new knowledge. They are, as Eyerman and Jamison (1991, p. 10) have said, "epistemic communities." They stress the historical and social construction of ideas and the active role that social movements play in knowledge production. Cognitive praxis, they argue, "does not come ready-made to a social movement. It is precisely in the creation, articulation, formulation of new thoughts and ideas—new knowledge—that a social movement defines itself in society" (p. 10). Knowledge is produced through debates over meeting agendas, the planning of meetings, campaigns and demonstrations, and exchanges over strategies and tactics. It is also generated, as Badat (1999) argues, in interaction with old movements, old traditions, concepts, and values and in the recombination and reinterpretation of intellectual roles and practices. The South African social movements through action over many years generated the hope and possibility of a new democratic, nonracial, and nonsexist order.

As we have seen, the social movements were molded within the particular historical conjunctures. The alliances across class, ethnicity, gender, and race forged organizational and educational practices. The setting of the agenda of the movements over time was shaped very directly by the economic conditions of the poor. They challenged the middle-class leadership of the ANC in the 1930s and 1940s and influenced directly what the movements did and how they operated. In the 1970s and 1980s, the organized working class strongly influenced what and how movements organized, but other working-class and poor people organizing in their localities contested this. Contestations among working-class and middle-class leadership were also reality. Old and new cultural forms shaped the movements' symbolic and expressive moments.

It is not possible to isolate the influence of class alone on the pedagogy and politics of social movements because class is so intertwined with other social categories. However, the social locations of the members and their relative degrees of wealth or poverty will, of course, have profound effects on their consciousness, which will shape what issues they take up and in whose interests they mobilize. For example, in the environmental movements in various parts of the world, there is at times deep difference of opinion between communities of environmental activists, depending on their socioeconomic circumstances. Some indigenous communities struggling for survival have sometimes asked whether an endangered animal is more significant than their endangered community.

So for adult educators and activists, this discussion on class and social movements raises several key questions:

- How is the mode of organizing within social movements going to encourage or inhibit people of different economic and social backgrounds from participating?
- Who is giving leadership? What are their socioeconomic circumstances? And how will this shape what issues the movement takes up when and where?
- What is the different cultural, ethnic, gender, and class mix of the social movement? How can the movement give expression to the range of cultural practices among women and men in order to maximize their participation?
- What are the historical class-related traditions within particular social movements that participants can build on?
- How does my own social and economic class position influence my own practices as adult educator and activist?

References

Abrahams, D. "South Africa: Social Movements, Coalitions, and the Struggle for Democracy." In Philippines-Canada Human Resource Development Program, *From Resistance to Transformation: Coalition Struggles in Canada, South Africa, the Philippines and Mexico.* Ontario: Philippines-Canada Human Resource Development Program, 1996.
Badat, S. *Black Student Politics, Higher Education and Apartheid: From SASO to SANSCO, 1968–1990.* Pretoria: HSRC, 1999.
Crowther, J., Martin, I., and Shaw, M. (eds.). *Popular Education and Social Movements in Scotland Today.* Leicester, England: National Institute of Adult Continuing Education, 1999.
Eyerman, R., and Jamison, A. *Social Movements: A Cognitive Approach.* Oxford: Polity Press, 1991.
Foley, G. *Learning in Social Action: A Contribution to Understanding Informal Education.* London: ZED Books, 1999.

62   CLASS CONCERNS

Hall, B., and Clover, D. "Social Movement Learning." In L. English (ed.), *International Encyclopedia of Adult Education*. London: Palgrave Macmillan, 2005.
Ismail, S. "A Poor Woman's Pedagogy." *Women's Studies Quarterly*, 2003, 31(3/4), 94–112.
Marshall, J. "Globalization from Below: Trade Union Connections." In S. Walters (ed.), *Globalization, Adult Education and Training: Impacts and Issues*. London: ZED Books, 1997.
Martin, I. "Introductory Essay: Popular Education and Social Movements in Scotland Today." In J. Crowther, I. Martin, and M. Shaw (eds.), *Popular Education and Social Movements in Scotland Today*. Leicester, England: National Institute of Adult Continuing Education, 1999.
Walters, S. *Education for Democratic Participation*. Bellville, South Africa: University of the Western Cape, 1989.
Walters, S., and Manicom, L. *Gender in Popular Education. Methods for Empowerment*. London: ZED Books, 1996.

SHIRLEY WALTERS is professor of adult and continuing education and director of the Division for Lifelong Learning at the University of Western Cape, South Africa. She has been active within South African social movements both as a scholar and activist over the past twenty-seven years.

7

Everyone is dependent on caring labor. Because women's labor is financially beneficial to global capitalism, gender is inseparable from class, regardless of the specific national or cultural contexts.

Class and Gender

Mechthild Hart

Class is neither a static notion, nor isolated from gender or other social categories. Rather, social class is mobile and fluid, both as a concept and as an experience. It also has a distinct economic underbelly that provides the connective tissue for the tremendously diverse experiences of class. Understanding the larger economic structure, that is, the unifying ground of a global capitalist system, is essential for getting a solid grip on the notion of class. Keeping its social and cultural dimension strongly wedded to its economic foundation makes related experiences more understandable, even more predictable.

Instead of giving an overview of the history and current uses of the manifold meanings of class in mainstream, leftist, or feminist discourse (which I have done elsewhere; see Hart, 2002), here I describe how the "layers of complexity and complicatedness" of class (Seabrook, 2002, p. 14) inform my educational practice. In some courses I teach class as an explicit theme; in others I weave it into the general investigation of the world economy and world trade organizations; in a course on research methods, I offer it as one of the topics students can explore, specifically in terms of their own interests and experiences. Here I describe core components of courses that in one way or another take up the political economy of women's work, thus constructing the blueprint of a course I am currently developing. My goals, approaches, and overall course designs are, however, shaped by the larger institutional framework within which they occur.

Where I Teach and Advise

The college where I have been teaching and mentoring for the past sixteen years is part of a private university, that is, a middle- to upper-class institu-

63

tion. Thinking about class therefore includes thinking about income, and I often wonder how students can possibly afford their education. The school's founders pledged to make higher education available and thus more afford-able to socially and economically disenfranchised groups; and its individu-alized, competence-based, interdisciplinary program for working adults definitely provides some structural support for this pledge. Students can earn credits for experiential learning at a fraction of equivalent tuition costs; the program requires fewer units to complete before graduation than any of the university's other programs; and it offers a particularly wide range of options for transferring courses from other colleges. The school also has a Bridge program with one of Chicago's city colleges. Before bridging over stu-dents can obtain competencies by taking Bridge classes at the city college.

In the not-so-distant past, most Bridge students could rely on tuition reimbursement from their employers, but since the cost-saving imperatives of the neoliberal economy started to take over, employers have become less generous. Students face higher education costs at the same time as they are losing any sense of job security. Most students have dependent children and levels of income that make them eligible for subsidized or unsubsidized fed-eral loans.

According to a report from the American Council on Education, "record shares of adults between ages 25 and 55 are now pursuing education," mainly in response to an "ever-changing job market" (Cook and King, 2004, p. 1). Although the study provides evidence for a link between postsecondary education and increased chances of earning a family-sustaining living wage, it is remarkably silent on a number of highly relevant, troublesome issues: that wealth and income inequality started to increase dramatically during the neoliberal good years (1980 to 1995) and that this trend is continuing; that corporate mergers and acquisitions extended the rise in unemployment from blue-collar workers to middle managers; that more and more temporary and part-time jobs are replacing permanent full-time jobs; and that low-wage, low-skill jobs are replacing high-skill, high-wage jobs, not to speak of the recent trend of outsourcing these jobs to cheaper labor countries (Hahnel, 1999). The labor market has not only been restructured, it has also become much more volatile.

I have learned to suspect major work-related reasons behind students missing classes or failing to do homework assignments. My suspicion that a student's sudden silence may be the symptom of a paralyzing anxiety about possibly being downsized away is often well-founded. A woman stu-dent may also sit in class silently because her day started thirteen hours ago, when she got herself and her children ready to go to work or school, and she now uses the quiet time in class to make mental lists of what she needs to do when she gets home. Another student who is close to graduation may cancel her appointment to discuss her final project because she has to take care of an ill parent. Job loss due to outsourcing may be the major reason behind a student's sudden disappearance from the program. Bridge students have additional worries. Many of them are economic migrants trying to escape the increasing impoverishment of their home countries, whose mounting debts are the result of structural adjustment policies that the International Monetary Fund (IMF) has imposed (Ellwood, 2002). The students are often too poor to stay in the Bridge program once they bridge over to other colleges and have to pay high tuition costs.

This is the context within which I address the following questions: How is gender at work in the construction, interpretation, and lived experience of the mobile, multicultural notion of class? How do these processes and experiences enter the classroom? How do they influence my course designs and pedagogical practices? How and under what conditions do they affect students' expectations and willingness or desire to learn?

The Labor of Care: Bringing Gender to Class

No matter how different cultures perceive and interpret bodily and psychological needs, all humans have them; to attend to them is the core of caring work. Caring for others reaches deeply into our bodies and souls, regardless of who does the work and for what reasons. Like class, caring comprises a web of social, cultural, psychological, and spiritual complexities. All over the globe, it is mostly women who assume primary responsibility for this kind of work, irrespective of the specific cultural or economic parameters within which it takes place. This is why gender is a category of such fundamental importance, no matter how it intersects with other categories or where—in what region, country, or hemisphere—its practical implications play out.

The majority of students at my school are women. All of them are in one way or another drawn into caring labor. They do the typical women's work of either taking care of children or aging parents (and sometimes both) in addition to the real work of providing financially for their families. Sometimes I hear from women students about their deliberate attempts to postpone having children in order to be able to focus on their careers, but I hear this only during private conversations in my office. In several of my courses, caring labor is an explicit theme; other students and I carefully, caringly, draw out related experiences, but only after the classroom has become a relatively safe place.

I follow several steps when trying to create an environment that is safe enough for students to tell stories about the way caring work affects them and how they struggle with the many physical and psychological burdens that the actual caring labor, or the power of expectations emanating from it, places on them. First, I give students written narratives of other women's experiences, deliberately including stories from women who are differently placed in U.S. society or the world. This provides points of connection between, for example, white students of Italian and black students of African descent or between students who grew up locally and those newly arrived from Trinidad. The narratives are also meant to assist students in laying the experiential groundwork for the subsequent task of slowly but steadily piecing together the overall (global) economic structure that translates gender-specific burdens and expectations into issues strongly related to class. I then ask students to think about the importance of care in their own lives, whether they are the main providers of care, who cares for their well-being or takes care of them, and what might be possible reasons for a care deficit in their lives (see Tronto, 1993, for related conceptual distinctions).

Students sometimes tell stories that are clearly filled with anguish and pain. Taking the next step, that is, reading critical theoretical pieces that paint a realistic picture of the capitalist world economy, frequently provokes a shift in the emotional life of the class. Students begin, for instance, to voice their disbelief, shock, or outrage at the way international trade organizations have been gutting the power of cherished U.S. democratic institutions. A ten-week course cannot do away with all the emotions it inevitably stirs up. Similar to Lange (2004), I am very conscious of the importance of coupling the emotional-intellectual work that criticizes and denounces with a restorative dimension. Placing caring work at the center of concern, taking it out of its devalued state, and investigating what makes it such easy prey for "corporate cannibalism" (Korten, 2001, p. 192) does to some extent counteract all the negative stuff that students sometimes complain about, stuff that has a tendency to bury the restorative, life-affirming dimension of caring labor. I explicitly set aside some course sections to investigate or celebrate this positive dimension, but I also ask students to remain attentive to this side of caring work throughout the course and to make corresponding observations in their course journals.

The Relational Web of Work

Another aspect I ask students to keep track of during the entire course—and note in their journals—is the way that gender plays out in their relationships to their employer, their coworkers, and the work they do at home. Whether they are male or female, black or white or any other color, single or married, employed or unemployed, with or without children, I guide all students to observe the more obvious but also more subtle or taken-for-granted ways in which gender may operate in their work lives. Not only does this approach embrace all the students in the course, it also nudges them away from the socially entrenched equation of work with employment.

Questions concerning individual identities loom large in these discussions. After we list social categories such as immigrant status, age, national origin, race, degree of ability or disability, or culture, I ask students which ones they would choose when asked to define their identity or identities and how they would describe some of the key indicators. We then look at the different ways that gender intersects with all the categories and corresponding identities, and the multilayered meanings and realities of the term *gender* emerge.

This process taps into deeply lodged emotions. It also requires students to engage in the intellectual-emotional effort of finding connections between highly charged social and individual realities, particularly in relation to corresponding kinds of discrimination. Some students are quite vocal about forms of gender-based discrimination that they witness at their workplace; others are more hesitant and more careful in recording incidents or making related observations. Sometimes male or female students claim that gender plays absolutely no role in their work lives. In a racially mixed class with a majority of white students, there is usually also a prolonged silence about racist or ethnocentrist kinds of discrimination; and when someone articulates them, gender remains hovering above related knowledge and experiences, waiting to be reined in to enrich the discussion at the appropriate times. I have learned to read patiently the different silences that punctuate these processes rather than filling them with teacher talk. A silence can speak very loudly about students' "loaded relationship to their course of study and their educational environment," but it can also "mark the places where students are making meaning" (Brooks and Cayetano, 1999, p. 62). As the course progresses and the more we insert experiential and analytical pieces in the gender-class puzzle, student agency moves from silence to written and spoken articulations of the meanings that they have made during stretches of silence.

We Are All Members of the Working Class

Once the protective or puzzled silences become less pronounced, the class is ready to move into the economic underside of the various kinds of discrimination we have identified so far. I start this process by supplying students with various statistics and numbers that demonstrate the growing divide between the rich and the poor, within the United States, and between countries in the northern and southern hemispheres. We then look at the stories and analyses we have produced so far and try to order them under the umbrella term *divisions of labor*. We look at excerpts from Collins's book *Fighting Words* (1998), in which she writes about slavery in the old global economy and the subsequent racialization of economic class relationships. Students also read the chapter "The Colour of Money: Race, Gender, and the Many Oppressions of Global Capital," in McNally's book *Another World Is Possible* (2002). By recording the history of old and new (neoliberal) globalization, the emergence of modern racism, and the predominance of women workers in modern sweatshops, McNally illustrates the interrelationship of "capitalism, patriarchy, and colonial rule" (p. 124). Patriarchy here emerges as an integral part of the global neocolonial capitalist system rather than as an issue of interest only to women.

Looking at the manifold divisions of labor (including the sexual division) also means looking at the rich diversity of working people all over the world. We therefore fill the faceless abstractions conjured up by the statistical renderings of inequality and poverty with the concrete conditions of ordinary people (Seabrook, 2002). By looking at what people actually do or create, we define *working class* as a function rather than a low social status.

Practically everyone teaching on the subject (see, for instance, the contributions to Linkon, 1999) has observed the fact that people shy away from identifying themselves as members of the working class. Seabrook (2002) gives a wonderful historical account of the changing meaning of *working class* in political or academic discourses; discusses why the term has disappeared from sight; and explores how this contributes to the shameful, constant undercurrent of its multiple, pluralist meanings. Once we translate the term *working class* into a myriad of productive, wealth-creating activities, students become ready to let the specter out of the working-class closet. We can then probe a bit more into the notion of the middle class and how or why it signifies a socially valued status rather than a particular function. It does not take long before everyone in class chuckles and agrees that they are all members of the working class. So breaking down the idea of class into its constitutive activities allows it to be more readily appreciated.

Mobile Capital, Mobile Motherhood

In order to better understand the structural connections between class and gender, we now look at what we previously learned about caring labor and how being financially devalued is the counterside of being superexploited. By shifting our attention from the realities of domestic work to the domestic worker herself, we arrive at a point at which we can bring together the social, economic, political, and ideological components of gender and class. An orientation toward needs rather than profit represents a common ground for all kinds of caring labor. Cultural, political, and economic differences among women determine who does this work and who pays for it. We therefore examine what it means when paid and unpaid domestic labor take place within the same household. Although with pronouncedly different tasks and responsibilities, the female employer and her domestic worker are clearly ensconced in a class relationship. Moreover, the new world order continues the U.S. history of racialized paid domestic labor but now on a global scale. Domestic workers are part of a growing global market for feminized export labor (see, for instance, Gamburd, 2000; Pyle and Ward, 2003).

At this point it is unavoidable to address the new world order's shift from productive to various forms of extractive capital investment. Many of my students work for banks, insurance companies, and other financial institutions; and they know a lot about stock indexes, hedge funds, or derivatives. I can count on at least one student willing to assist me in my attempt to explain terms such as the *debt pyramid* or *junk bonds* and to lecture on why and how investment capital keeps flitting across the globe at lightning speed. Where "for every U.S. dollar circulating in the real economy, $25–50 circulate in the world of pure finance" (Petras and Veltmeyer, 2001, p. 15), investments are delinked from the actual production of wealth, that is, the real economy (see also Cavanagh and Mander, 2002; Ellwood, 2002; Korten, 2001; McNally, 2002). To borrow a term that lies at the core of Marx's analysis of class relations, the new relations to the means of extraction are not different, only more dangerous, more life-threatening than the relations of older ones to the means of production. A capitalist world economy that is driven by financial markets lives off a dynamic instability that affects the lives of all people, working or nonworking. This economy dislocates more and more people, causes the loss of millions of jobs, and destroys social and environmental conditions for survival.

Extractive capitalism now includes the extraction of emotional and sexual resources (Hochschild, 2002). Who is taking care of the children that the export laborer, the mobile mother, left behind? This work remains in the economic netherland of the private sphere, where grandmothers or other female relatives support the superexploitation of exported caring labor in a private household somewhere else. Migrant domestic workers move from the poor southern hemisphere to the rich northern hemisphere, where they often become an inevitable and affordable necessity for gainfully employed middle-class women. Export laborers' remittances support their families left behind, and they provide the hard currency that the sending country desperately needs in order to be able to pay its debts to the IMF or World Bank. Sending countries, such as the Philippines, had to accept IMF "conditions" by privatizing public enterprises and public services and by cutting or eliminating public funds for health care and food subsidies. Women thus service their country's public debts by exporting their caring labor, and as domestic workers they directly service private bodily needs in their host country (Pyle and Ward, 2003; Sassen, 2002).

When students begin to see that women's work is economically quite beneficial to global capitalism and that it is therefore inseparable from the notion of class, racial, ethnic, or cultural identity, they are ready to revisit their own lived experiences and investigate how these may fit into this larger system. I sometimes ask them to draw an image that translates the superexploitability and thus profitability of caring labor into an image of the individual and cultural importance of caring for life on this planet. This exercise produces wonderful results, demonstrating that students are fully aware of the creative and life-sustaining dimension of caring labor. It also provides points of connection among students whose particular group affiliations may relate to each other in rather conflictual ways but who nevertheless agree on the importance of a kind of labor that gives to rather than extracts from life.

Where Do We Go from Here?

Many students at my school have already experienced or are facing downward mobility. In order to get a college degree, they shoulder additional financial burdens and invest tremendous amounts of time and energy, and this at a time when a college degree no longer guarantees success (Aronson, 1999). Brooks and Cayetano (1999) therefore challenge critical educators who claim solidarity with working-class people to ask some unsettling economic questions: What is this for? Where are we going? How are we getting there?

These are huge questions, and trying to find answers seems an impossible task. Nevertheless, the particular context within which we do our educational work may at least give us some clues about where to go in order to find possible answers. I found some of the clues in Luttrell's study (1997), which addresses various social and epistemological differences between being schoolsmart and motherwise. These terms, coined by the women in her study, are packed with a host of normative assumptions about gender, race, and class; and they unfold into a myriad of related hierarchical relations, not only across but also within these categories. These hierarchies always signify unequal distributions of responsibilities that specifically affect women, especially those with children. Consequently, when the women go to school, they have to navigate "between dirty dishes and polished discourse" (Ferretti, 1999, p. 69) and between their paid and unpaid work.

Teaching and learning about connections between nannies, maids, and sex workers (Ehrenreich and Hochschild, 2002) on the one hand and polished discourses on the other means undermining the relations of knowledge production that reign supreme in higher education institutions. A participatory, process-conscious pedagogy that investigates the manifold meanings of class and gender and draws on the knowledge of motherwise people inevitably redistributes the means of knowledge production. It is a pedagogy that deliberately creates spaces for acknowledging and affirming the fact that everyone is in need of, dependent on caring labor, thus also undermining the class-based dualism between intellectual and physical labor. Schoolsmart academics cannot and should not replace the outsider knowledge of motherwise people but can nevertheless be of tremendous use for the intellectual work of critique and analysis that lays bare specific forms of social and economic exploitation. In all my courses, I therefore try to employ a pedagogy in which class and gender may not always be the main themes but in which we turn upside down class- and gender-based divisions of labor and corresponding dualistic ways of seeing and living in the world. It is a pedagogy that counteracts and affirms, criticizes and replenishes, hopefully giving students the necessary strength to pursue their struggles beyond the classroom walls.

References

Aronson, A. "Reversals of Fortune: Downward Mobility and the Writing of Nontraditional Students." In S. L. Linkon (ed.), *Teaching Working Class*. Amherst: University of Massachusetts Press, 1999.

Brooks, J., and Cayetano, F. "The (Dis)Location of Culture: On the Way to Literacy." In S. L. Linkon (ed.), *Teaching Working Class.* Amherst: University of Massachusetts Press, 1999.

Cavanagh, J., and Mander, J. (eds.). *Alternatives to Economic Globalization: A Better World Is Possible.* San Francisco: Berrett-Koehler, 2002.

Collins, P. H. *Fighting Words: Black Women and the Search for Justice.* Minneapolis: University of Minnesota Press, 1998.

Cook, B., and King, J. E. *Low-Income Adults in Profile: Improving Lives Through Higher Education.* Washington, D.C.: American Council on Education, 2004.

Ehrenreich, B., and Hochschild, A. R. (eds.). *Global Woman: Nannies, Maids, and Sex Workers in the New Economy.* New York: Metropolitan Books, 2002.

Ellwood, W. *The No-Nonsense Guide to Globalization.* Oxford: New Internationalist Publications, 2002.

Ferretti, E. "Between Dirty Dishes and Polished Discourse: How Working-Class Moms Construct Student Identities." In S. L. Linkon (ed.), *Teaching Working Class.* Amherst: University of Massachusetts Press, 1999.

Gamburd, M. R. *The Kitchen Spoon's Handle: Transnationalism and Sri Lanka's Migrant Housemaids.* Ithaca: Cornell University Press, 2000.

Hahnel, R. *Panic Rules: Everything You Need to Know About the Global Economy.* Boston: South End Press, 1999.

Hart, M. *The Poverty of Life-Affirming Work: Motherwork, Education, and Social Change.* Westport, Conn.: Greenwood Press, 2002.

Hochschild, A. R. "Love and Gold." In B. Ehrenreich and A. R. Hochschild (eds.), *Global Woman: Nannies, Maids, and Sex Workers in the New Economy.* New York: Metropolitan Books, 2002.

Korten, D. C. *When Corporations Rule the World.* San Francisco: Berrett-Koehler, 2001.

Lange, E. A. "Transformative and Restorative Learning: A Vital Dialectic for Sustainable Societies." *Adult Education Quarterly,* 2004, *54*(2), 121–139.

Linkon, S. L. (ed.). *Teaching Working Class.* Amherst: University of Massachusetts Press, 1999.

Luttrell, W. *Schoolsmart and Motherwise: Working-Class Women's Identity and Schooling.* New York: Routledge, 1997.

McNally, D. *Another World Is Possible: Globalization and Anti-Capitalism.* Winnipeg, Canada: Arbeiter Ring, 2002.

Petras, J., and Veltmeyer, H. *Globalization Unmasked: Imperialism in the Twenty-First Century.* Halifax, Canada: Fernwood, 2001.

Pyle, J. L., and Ward, K. B. "Recasting Our Understanding of Gender and Work During Global Restructuring." *International Sociology,* 2003, *18*(3), 461–489.

Sassen, S. "Global Cities and Survival Circuits." In B. Ehrenreich and A. R. Hochschild (eds.), *Global Woman: Nannies, Maids, and Sex Workers in the New Economy.* New York: Metropolitan Books, 2002.

Seabrook, J. *The No-Nonsense Guide to Class, Caste and Hierarchies.* Oxford: New Internationalist Publications, 2002.

Tronto, J. C. *Moral Boundaries: A Political Argument for an Ethic of Care.* New York: Routledge, 1993.

MECHTHILD HART is professor at DePaul University's School for New Learning in Chicago, Illinois.

8

This chapter argues that a critical analysis of the inter-
locking notions of class, race, and gender is needed to
enable adult education to respond to growing inequalities.

Class and Race

Shahrzad Mojab

Adult education in Western societies emerged in the course of the struggle over how best to help the working class to learn about, engage in, and act on capitalist relations of production. By the time industrial capitalism was developing in the late eighteenth century in Western Europe and North America, only a minority of the male aristocratic, middle-class, and clerical population had access to formal, literate education. Industrial capitalism was the first social and economic formation to depend on a literate, formally educated, skilled labor force. However, exploiting the cheap labor of children, women, slaves, and people of color, capitalism itself was initially an obstacle to the spread of universal education.

Reacting to the conditions of appalling poverty created by the most powerful production system the world had seen, social movements, especially those of workers and women, as well as groups and individuals including churches, educators, artists, journalists, politicians, and political parties, advocated universal education for both genders, all age groups, and citizens belonging to different classes, races, and religions. The struggle over adult education in the past as in the present has involved conflicting political, ideological, and pedagogical tendencies.

Some schools wanted to provide the working class with education for its own sake; others sought to combine the notion of knowledge for the sake of knowledge with trade union skills. Meanwhile, there was a growing emphasis on the value of vocational education and the creation of an efficient labor force. In these competing tendencies, various religious groups also had their eyes on improving the conditions of the working class (Simon, 1990; Spencer and McIlroy, 1988). In most of these efforts, (working) class was reified as the physical labor of a white male worker. It is within this historical, monolithic, or unidimensional conceptualization of

NEW DIRECTIONS FOR ADULT AND CONTINUING EDUCATION, no. 106, Summer 2005 © Wiley Periodicals, Inc. 73

the notion of class that adult education overlooks other significant social determinants such as race and gender in shaping class position.

This chapter is a study of the dialectical relationship between race and class as it pertains to adult education epistemology, pedagogy, and practice. It provides a class analysis of race and racism, paying attention to interlocking notions of race, gender, and class. I will argue that a critical class, race, and gender analysis is needed to enable adult education as a field and adult educators as its practitioners to respond to the growing inequalities in the world. I will also exhibit, based on my own pedagogical practice, ways to integrate notions of class and race into adult education pedagogy and practice.

Dialectics as a Method of Inquiry on Race, Racism, and Class

Like other concepts, class, race, gender, and capitalism are highly contested even among socialists, feminists, anticolonialists, or anticapitalists who find them indispensable (for an extensive literature review, see Murphy, 2004). A host of theoretical positions ranging from liberalism to poststructuralism have either discarded one or more of these concepts or have privileged one over the other. Moving from these theoretical positions to those that find concepts of class, race, and gender relevant to the understanding of the capitalist world, we find a great divide in theorizations and dialectical analyses. The former treat classes as groupings based on income, status, or rank; the latter depict classes as "large groups of people differing from each other by the place they occupy in a historically determined system of social production, by their relation (in most cases fixed and formulated in law) to the means of production, by their role in the social organization of labour, and consequently, by the dimensions of the share of social income of which they dispose and the mode of acquiring it" (Lenin, [1919] 1965, p. 421).

Theorized as both social and historical, capitalist relations of production constitute a social formation distinct from previous ones, although like all systems it has both to produce and reproduce. According to Marx ([1867] 1977), "[a] society can no more cease to produce than it can cease to consume. When viewed therefore, as a connected whole, and in the constant flux of its incessant renewal, every social process of production is at the same time a process of reproduction" (p. 711). In other words, capitalism "produces not only commodities, not only surplus value, but it also produces and reproduces the capital relation itself; on the one hand the capitalist, on the other the wage-labourer" (p. 724).

In this dialectical theorization, classes are not accidental or readily shifting aggregates of people stratified along the lines of employment, rank, income, or life chances. They are, rather, crucial constituents of the capitalist social, economic, ideological, and epistemological formation. Class, in Marxist theory, provides dividing lines not only in the distribution of economic power but also in epistemology, ontology, ideology, philosophy, and politics. From this perspective class struggle involves much more than economic conflict between workers and capitalists. Some argue, in fact, that workers' struggle for economic welfare alone offers nothing more than a perpetuation of capitalism. One may argue that education too is a component of this vicious circle of reproducing capitalism. The dialectical method allows us to move out of the circle by seeing consciousness (agency) and matter (capitalism) as the unity and struggle of opposites, forming not a dichotomy or binarism but rather a dialectical contradiction in which the two sides co-occur, coexist, collide, and are capable of negating each other (for more on dialectical materialism, see Gibson, 1993; Ollman, 1993, 1998).

The reproduction of capitalism could probably be less complicated if class had constituted the only source of the unequal division of power. It happens that societies are divided also along the lines of gender, race, language, religion, nationality, and ethnicity, to name only a few historical cleavages. Even more significant is the interlocking of these contradictions in ways that both threaten and strengthen the (re)production process. In the absence of a dialectical approach, however, methodological individualism and theoretical atomism, both traditional or postmodernist, treat race and class as largely unrelated. Although the trinity of race-gender-class appears in the literature, one strong tendency in recent years has been a retreat from class and descent into discourse, identity, language, and desire. Although these various theoretical turns and twists have broadened our view of the intricacies of gender and race relations, the exclusion of class has, I believe, obscured the ways in which the social and economic formation of capitalism draws the contours of the struggle for power. In the absence of class perspectives, race- and gender-centered theories are in a difficult position to advocate nonracist and nonsexist positions.

In light of this theoretical discussion, we may ask how adult education stands in relation to the racialized and genderized capitalist economy. We may note, for instance, that adult education depends on capitalism; it is nurtured by it; it educates adults to serve the capitalist market economy; it contributes to the (re)production of the capitalist system (for more on this point, see Allman, 1999, 2001). The adult education literature that treats relations of race and class dialectically is indeed quite limited. Most of the research is focused on diversity, marginality as social location outside of class, and transformation as a strategy to change unequal relations of power (Butterwick, Fenwick, and Mojab, forthcoming; Hayes and Colin, 1994; Johnson-Bailey, 2001; Quinnan, 1997).

Radical Pedagogy of Race and Class

Gibson's categorization of the pedagogy of race into two types of liberal and critical approaches is an important contribution to the dialectical understanding of race and class. He argues that, in the liberal tradition, racism is a set of attitudes or ideas that targets racial and ethnic groups and denies them dignity, humanity, or equality. It is a deviation from the democratic tradition and rooted in ignorance. This attitudinal problem, liberal tradition argues, can be solved through changing the mind of the individual through education and promotion of diversity, pluralism, and multiculturalism. By contrast, a dialectical perspective looks at race and racism as socially and historically constructed phenomena and as forms of the exercise of power that enter into complex relationships with the exercise of class and gender power.

In a racially divided society, in which power is divided along the lines of class and gender, membership in the dominant racial group confers power on the individual. Even when constitutions and charters of rights emphasize the equality of citizens before the law (as they do in North America, Western Europe, Australia, or New Zealand), the extralegal inequality of races dwarfs the much celebrated formal equality that the civic nation grants. If race is a source of social and political power, this power has to be exercised. If racial relations constitute a social system, this system has to produce the conditions of its own reproduction, that is, race, racism, and racialized relations. Racial power is exercised every time aboriginal peoples, people of African descent, blacks, or members of visible minority groups experience racism in their everyday encounters with the dominant race. Reproducing these relations requires ideological and epistemological frameworks that naturalize the unequal division of racial power.

In the wake of the antiracist struggles of the 1960s, we have a growing body of critical knowledge on pedagogy produced by feminists, antiracist educators, and others, which suggests alternative ways of learning, relating, and knowing (Anderson and Collins, 1992; Bannerji, 1993; Dei, 1996; Dua and Robertson, 1999; Calliste and Dei, 2000; hooks, 1990; Jensen, 1998). Nevertheless, we have not yet been able to make a radical breakthrough, and I doubt very much whether such a rupture in pedagogy will be coming soon. In order to contextualize this claim, I will retell two of my pedagogical tales.

Being Minority and Teaching Minority. I taught a third-year sociology course called "Minority-Majority Relations" years ago. I was the last-minute substitute. The course was part of the curriculum for a long time. The calendar description and the outline that I inherited took a traditional anthropological approach to the topic; it advocated an appreciation for the multicultural nature of Canadian society and gave a descriptive account of the role of these cultures in building Canada as a nation and the current aspirations of these diverse communities. The course, as handed down to me, was not sensitive to critical analyses of power dynamics, which, I believe, shapes and defines majority-minority relations. Neither was it informed by the rich body of scholarship on the intersections of feminism and antiracism. Overhauling the course was not an easy task, especially within a short period of time. It was also considered to be an issue-based course, as distinct from general and theory-oriented topics. As a minority woman, I was the right type to teach such a course. Bannerji (1995, p. 230) articulates this experience by stating, "I still notice how I, and a few more of 'us' who work at the university, have to teach these 'issue' courses, or better still how our courses even when they have a highly theoretical organization are considered as being 'issue' based."

Nevertheless, I took the task on and redesigned the course with three principles in mind. First, a course on minority-majority relations must be contextualized within the Canadian histories of colonization of the aboriginal peoples, the expansion of capitalist relations of production, and the role of immigrants in building the nation-state of Canada. Second, this historical contextualization should interweave race, gender, and class relations. Third, critiquing the unequal relations of domination is not enough, however; it does not even constitute a radical pedagogy (for an excellent discussion on what constitutes critical theories, see Griffin and Moffat, 1997). The course must introduce alternatives to the existing power relations. Critique and alternatives to the status quo may better challenge students to reflect, act, and resist.

The course started with more than fifty students; after the first class, the number dropped to about thirty. Among them were only three women of color, the rest of the class consisting of white women and men. The number of white male students declined substantially as the course progressed. As is my teaching practice, I conducted an informal anonymous survey during the first class in order to get to know the students better, to incorporate their interests into the course, to satisfy their expectations, and to understand their reasons for taking the course. The result of the survey indicated the challenge that I had to face for the rest of the term. Some students indicated their hesitation about the content of the course as being too ideological and mentioned that they would take a wait-and-see approach and wish for a more balanced view. Others were less polite and made outright racist or sexist remarks. For instance, in answering the question "What do you hope to learn in this class?" a student wrote, "to learn how to pronounce your name"; another wrote "how such a small woman made it." A major theme in the students' response was the sense of guilt about the exclusion of others and, thus, they hoped to learn "what is this all about." One student wrote, "I don't like the term *racial minority*. It sounds negative."

In order to have the pulse of the class, after each class I asked students to write an anonymous one-minute paper. This exercise has been one of the most illuminating teaching techniques that I have used. It brings out the hidden feeling and emotion of those who are allowing the class to challenge their consciousness, values, and social learning and feeling motivated enough to make difficult choices. Most of the students appreciated the opportunity to express themselves freely through these little writings. However, I was not surprised to see that they wrote mostly on the topic of intersection between violence and racism and sexism. A student wrote, "If to sum up the class . . . it was not much more than fucking male-bashing. This is not because it personally offended me, but that it lacked rational thought by some." Another student explained her or his disbelief in the following words: "However one must question the validity and reliability of information. . . . I feel that women are not a commodity in a contemporary democratic Western society; there is always going to be abuse of power in society, but this is not to say that it is always against females." A student asked, "I don't understand 'racist attitudes have potential usefulness for those in power.' Is this implying that the government in power is disseminating racist ideas to maintain their power and the status quo?"

"Is There Sunshine in Your Life?" As a newly appointed tenure-track faculty member, I was asked to design an undergraduate course on antiracism education that later I called "Diversity with Dignity: Anti-racism Education and Practice." The department asked me to frame the course within the epistemology of the nexus between adult education theory and practice. This meant that the class should interweave theory and practice; that I should select and design course readings and activities in ways that engage students in reflection, action, and praxis in an integrated way. Here are some moments of my experience, which revealed a web of relations of conflict, domination, and resistance.

In an academic environment, where the established norm for a faculty member is neutrality and objectivity, some students felt that I was too political and too much of an activist. Another norm that I was violating was being critical; students often equated critique with destructive attitude and negativity. One day an older white male student interrupted me and exclaimed, "Do you ever get up and simply say, 'What beautiful sunshine!'? Is there sunshine in your life?" Bewildered by his comment, I asked him to explain. He added that my passion for social justice and change had overwhelmed him; he thought that the injustice in society was not as pervasive as I was trying to depict it. Pondering on his comments, I thought that when we, minority women, contextualize our daily experience, we do not make it easy for students to engage in a normal relationship with us. My focus on the inequality of power relations seemed to challenge students' assumptions about the normality of existing race and gender relations. Such assumptions are inscribed in these student comments: it is "common sense" knowledge that racism and sexism are not good; "things have always been like this"; or "I have never been told otherwise." Although some students were questioning antiracist learning, an active minority was interested in radical antiracism. The majority, however, remained less vocal and participated in the debates as the course was making progress.

These actions and interactions point to the rootedness of race in our understanding of the world. If there are class and gender standpoints and epistemologies (Harding 2004), race also comes with its epistemologies and worldviews. Epistemological racism allow us to be "strongly anti-racist in our minds but be promulgating racism in profound ways we do not understand" (Scheurich and Young, 1997, p. 12). Looking at this relationship dialectically, one may see it as a contradiction between consciousness and matter. In other words, we are just beginning to understand the exercise of racial power in epistemology, a step forward, which if translated into pedagogy, amounts to an effort to transform consciousness into matter, that is, changing the material reality of racial domination through a more complex understanding of its dynamics.

Theoretical Tools for Transforming the Practice of Race and Class Pedagogy

People quite often view education as a powerful means for changing the individual and society. Seeing it as a force of progress, they overlook its contradictory role of reproducing the status quo. In the same vein, people of color, once present on the campus either as faculty members or students, act in conflicting ways. They act both as agents of change and agents of the status quo. It is difficult to understand the innumerable factors that contribute to the formation of such conflicting roles. I locate my pedagogy in the critical perspectives whose goal is to raise consciousness, that is, the realization that our problems—poverty, racism, sexism, oppression, violence, or injustice—are social constructions that society can dismantle and eradicate.

Although educating citizens about the perils of racism is apparently more effective than the legal regulation of race relations, neither education nor law can put an end to the exercise of racial power. Indeed, modern nation-states declare that all citizens are equal before the law irrespective of religion, sex, national origin, race, language, and so on. This is the Enlightenment idea of the separation of state and religion, state and ethnicity, state and gender, state and descent, state and race, and even state and language. Although in the past two or three decades many constitutions have enshrined these separations of power, the modern nation-state continues to exercise class (capitalism), gender (patriarchal), and racial power (white race in the West; see, for example, Goldberg, 2002). Racism, even when not enshrined in law in racially divided Western societies, continues to be one form of the exercise of power. In the racially segregated United States, for example, the federal state sent troops to escort African American students to a high school in Little Rock, Arkansas, in 1957 and to the University of Alabama in 1963. Forty years later the ruling Republican party had African Americans as national security advisor and secretary of state. The government continues to be a racial institution, however. The United States made racial profiling illegal not long ago but reinstated it as a policy under conditions it perceived as a threat to its national security after September 11, 2001. Although affirmative action reforms may change the appearance of the racial state, they cannot uproot racial domination.

Since the end of the Cold War, incessant massacres, genocides, war crimes, and crimes against humanity have been identified as ethnic, racial, national, and religious conflicts. Although such cleavages have always provided grounds for conflict, people rarely question the reduction of these ongoing tragedies to issues of race, ethnicity, and religion. In the absence of class analysis and with the discounting of capitalism as a source of conflict, the contemporary world seems to be ruled only by racial and ethnic hatred. Works such as *World on Fire: How Exporting Free Market Democracy Breeds Ethnic Hatred and Global Instability* (Chua, 2003), which detect class and economic interests behind racial and ethnic wars, remain largely unnoticed. The current intellectual and theoretical privileging of difference works against the long and powerful traditions of internationalism. Racism, nativism, nationalism, and ethnocentrism may be at work when nonwhites and non-Westerners reduce Marxism, feminism, secularism, or internationalism to white discourses. In spite of its rootedness in social movements based on solidarity, adult education in the past twenty years has been reshaped by such conformist theorizations of power, which push difference rather than domination or marginalization rather than oppression onto the center stage.

No doubt adult educators, as conscious human beings, are engaged in intervening in the status quo. They see the ways in which capitalism creates jobs and at the same time destroys them, how this system needs skilled labor but also deskills them (Mojab, 2001). In its pursuit of profit, capitalism has little if any regard for the dignity, happiness, safety, and security of those who constitute the labor force. The capitalist corporation is now a legal person more powerful than the human individual (Bakan, 2004). In our time globalization is draining the educational system and its resources and is redefining its goals. There is no job security for the majority and less stability even for a short time. The anarchy of capitalist production (production depends on making profit in an uncertain, risky, competitive environment, which no one can plan or predict) and the growing pace of the movement of capital (layoffs, downsizing, or outsourcing) challenge education and educators at all levels. "Everything solid melts into the air," to quote Marx (Marx and Engels, [1848] 1954, p. 20), and does so hourly and daily. Globalizing and privatizing capital has already transformed many governments in the West into its servants; it has similar demands on (adult) education. The slogan is: "All power to the market!" Education has to follow suit. There is thus a struggle over redefining adult education.

I see in the latest international declaration on the goals of adult education a struggle between adult educators and the state-market bloc (see the text of Mid-term Review of CONFINTEA, 2003, and the 1997 Hamburg Declaration on Adult Learning [both available from the UNESCO Institute for Education Web site]). Although the declaration confirms conditions for the reproduction of the capitalist system, it also resists the dehumanizing and alienating demands of capitalism. From a dialectical perspective, one should look at the conditions that have restrained capitalism as well as the resistances that it generates. In spite of its dual nature, why has it remained a piece of paper or at best a document filed away in bureaucracies and academic libraries?

Adult educators, like everyone else, are not totally free from the constraints of necessity. I am confirming here that freedom exists in unity and conflict with necessity (existing conditions, the status quo). Freedom consists in understanding and transforming necessity. To put it differently, we have the knowledge and resources to change the dominant genderized, racialized, and class-based relations of power. It is thus relevant to ask why education, with all the might it has gathered since the industrial revolution, is unable to change the social relations of ruling (Smith, 1987). Why do educators and much of the rest of the intellectual establishment who find it expedient to reiterate the discourses of race, ethnicity, and religion not hesitate to declare the end of the working class, the end of the critique of capitalism, and to ignore concepts such as oppression, exploitation, and socialism?

I have tried to provide a class and race analysis of the state of adult education. I have argued that adult education, as it is practiced in the West, contributes to the reproduction of capitalist social relations, a social formation that combines unprecedented powers of construction and destruction. If the overoptimistic Enlightenment educators believed that education can do it all, I point to the interconnectedness of all sites of struggle. If during the Enlightenment, the end of the horrors of the medieval world was visible in the promises of capitalism, educators today need to contemplate the end of two centuries of actually existing capitalism.

References

Allman, P. *Revolutionary Social Transformation: Democratic Hopes, Political Possibilities and Critical Education.* New York: Bergin & Garvey, 1999.

Allman, P. *Critical Education Against Global Capitalism: Karl Marx and Revolutionary Critical Education.* New York: Bergin & Garvey, 2001.

Anderson, M. L., and Collins, P. H. (eds.). *Race, Class, and Gender: An Anthology.* Belmont, Calif.: Wadsworth, 1992.

Bakan, J. *The Corporation: The Pathological Pursuit of Profit and Power.* Toronto: Viking Canada, 2004.

Bannerji, B. "Re: Turning the Gaze." In S. Richer and L. Weir (eds.), *Beyond Political Correctness: Toward the Inclusive University.* Toronto: University of Toronto Press, 1995.

Bannerji, H. (ed.). *Returning the Gaze: Essays on Racism, Feminism, and Politics.* Toronto: Sisters Vision, 1993.

Butterwick, S., Fenwick, T., and Mojab, S. "Canadian Research in Adult Education in the 1990s: A Cautious Cartography." *Adult Education Quarterly,* forthcoming.

Calliste, A., and Dei, G. S. (eds.). *Anti-Racist Feminism: Critical Race and Gender Studies.* Halifax: Fernwood, 2000.

Chua, A. *World on Fire: How Exporting Free Market Democracy Breeds Ethnic Hatred and Global Instability.* New York: Doubleday, 2003.

Dei, G. S. *Anti-Racism Education: Theory and Practice.* Halifax: Fernwood, 1996.

Dua, E., and Robertson, A. (eds.). *Scratching the Surface: Canadian Anti-Racist Feminist Thought.* Toronto: Women's Press, 1999.

Gibson, R. "Dialectical Materialism—For the Earnest." [http://www.pipeline.com/~rgibson/diamata.html]. 1993.

Gibson, R. "On Racism: Idealist and Materialist Approaches." [http://www.pipeline.com/~rgibson/approach.htm]. 1995.

Goldberg, D. T. *The Racial State.* Cambridge, Mass.: Blackwell, 2002.

Griffin, S. M., and Moffat, C. L. (eds.). *Radical Critiques of the Law.* Kansas: University Press of Kansas, 1997.

Harding, S. (ed.). *The Feminist Standpoint Theory Reader: Intellectual and Political Controversies.* New York: Routledge, 2004.

Hayes, E., and Colin III, S.A.J. (eds.). *Confronting Racism and Sexism.* New Directions for Adult and Continuing Education, no. 61. San Francisco: Jossey-Bass, 1994.

hooks, b. *Yearning: Race, Gender, and Cultural Politics.* Toronto: Between the Lines, 1990.

Jensen, R. "White Privilege Shapes the U.S." *Baltimore Sun,* July 19, 1998, p. 1C.

Johnson-Bailey, J. "The Power of Race and Gender: Black Women's Struggle and Survival in Higher Education." In R. M. Cervero and A. L. Wilson (eds.), *Power in Practice: Adult Education and the Struggle for Knowledge and Power in Society.* San Francisco: Jossey-Bass, 2001.

Lenin, V. I. "A Great Beginning." *Collected Works,* vol. 29. (Y. Sdobnikov, trans.) Moscow: Progress, 1965. (Originally published 1919.)

Marx, K. *Capital.* (F. Engels, ed.; S. Moore and E. Aveling, trans.) London: Lawrence and Wishart, 1977. (Originally published 1867.)

Marx, K., and Engels, F. *The Communist Manifesto.* (S. Moore, trans.) Chicago: Henry Regnery Co., 1954. (Originally published 1848.)

Mojab, S. "The Power of Economic Globalization: Deskilling Immigrant Women Through Training." In R. M. Cervero and A. L. Wilson (eds.), *Power in Practice.* San Francisco: Jossey-Bass, 2001.

Murphy, M. "RaceSci: History of Race in Science." [http://www.racesci.org]. Accessed October 2004.

Ollman, B. *Dialectical Investigations.* New York: Routledge, 1993.

Ollman, B. "Why Dialectics? Why Now?" *Science and Society,* 1998, 62(3), 338–357.

Quinnan, T. W. *Adult Students "At-Risk": Culture Bias in Higher Education.* New York: Bergin & Garvey, 1997.

Scheurich, J. S., and Young, M. D. "Coloring Epistemologies: Are Our Research Epistemologies Racially Biased?" *Educational Researcher,* 1997, 26(4), 4–16.

Simon, B. (ed.). *The Search for Enlightenment: The Working Class and Adult Education in the Twentieth Century.* Leicester, England: Lawrence and Wishart, 1990.

Smith, D. *The Everyday World as Problematic: A Feminist Sociology.* Toronto: Toronto University Press, 1987.

Spencer, B., and McIlroy, J. *University Adult Education in Crisis.* Leeds: University of Leeds, Leeds Studies in Adult Education, 1988.

UNESCO Institute for Education. "CONFINTEA Mid-term Review." [http://www.unesco.org/education/uie]. Accessed October 2004.

UNESCO Institute for Education. "Hamburg Declaration on Adult Learning." [http://www.unesco.org/education/uie]. Accessed October 2004.

SHAHRZAD MOJAB is associate professor in the Department of Adult Education and Counselling Psychology at the Ontario Institute for Studies in Education of the University of Toronto, and the director of the Institute for Women's Studies and Gender Studies, University of Toronto.

9

In summarizing earlier arguments for privileging a class perspective on adult education, this chapter considers that perspective's practical relevance and suggests resources for further reading.

The Continued Relevance of Class

Tom Nesbit

Whatever its particular focus, approach, or clientele, adult education is an essentially political project. The struggles for power—who has it, how they use it, and in whose interests—lie at the heart of the adult education enterprise. Concerned with identity and personal and social change, adult education seeks to provide the knowledge, skills, and attitudes for people to engage more fully in their individual and social worlds. And it's in the political realm, encompassing both the individual and the social, that the effects of class are most clearly visible.

So adult educators, professional people engaged with most aspects of human endeavor, need to appreciate and understand the complexities of class. Such an approach offers two immediate benefits. First, it helps "subvert the tendency to focus only on the thoughts, attitudes, and experiences of those who are materially privileged" (hooks, 2000, p. 185). Second, it benefits learners. As Linkon (1999, p. 6) claims, "the more we can recognize and understand working-class culture, the more clearly we can recognize the strengths of our working-class students and, more important, the better our chances of engaging and inspiring them."

Previous chapters clearly illustrate how class, adult education, and social power are closely interwoven. They also emphasize the salient and dynamic nature of class: it is everywhere, not given but made and remade through people's everyday actions. Thus, class manifests itself in and is part of the material and social conditions of daily life. Class affects the places where people live and work, the jobs they do, their sources of income and wealth, the things on which and the way in which they spend that income, their health, and the relationships they have with others. Class also affects the interior world of thoughts and feelings and the way that people experience material reality. In Sennett's words (1999, p. 10), people's position in the economic order influences their "character": those "personal traits we value in ourselves and for which we seek to be valued by others." Class also influences both educational and political involvement, in many cases disproportionately (Offe, 1985). Participation in educational and political activities diminishes among those with lower economic status: "The very nature of working-class life—with its connotations of limited resources, instability and insecurity, limited education, and relative powerlessness in the workplace—has exacerbated for workers the kind of political disengagement that sometimes reverberates beyond the boundaries of the working class" (Croteau, 1995, p. xiv). To put it another way: the poor have little public voice.

These issues should trouble adult educators, particularly those concerned with social justice and emancipation. The preceding chapters suggest that the intersections of social class and adult education can provide important areas for reflection, study, and further action. They also show that class offers a lens through which to examine many of the important issues currently affecting adult education. In this final chapter, I first summarize the arguments for privileging a class perspective on adult education. Next, I consider the practical importance of adopting such a perspective and then conclude with some suggestions for further reading.

The Importance of a Class Perspective

As earlier chapters suggest, class can mean different things to different people: a theoretical device for analyzing the social world; shared social conditions; or a set of particular orientations, beliefs, and life practices. Popular understandings of class still describe it in terms of jobs, income, wealth, the lifestyles that people can buy, or the power that accrues from ownership. Yet as several chapters show, class is less a possession than a dynamic: a relationship between different people and groups divided along axes of power and privilege. So class differences play out in power relations. And education plays a critical role in forming and mediating these relations: providing opportunities for personal mobility while legitimating social inequality. Thus, adopting a class perspective on adult education does two things: it draws clear links between educational institutions, the world of work, and the economic system that underpins them; and it highlights how educational institutions function to maintain and inculcate societal ideology and values.

Many adult educators find such a perspective overwhelming and offputting. Others question the extent to which adult educators should critique dominant social systems and the prevailing capitalist system. Yet the many and varied ways that class shapes adult education continue to demand our attention. First, as Rubenson's chapter and Apple (1990, 1995) and others have cogently argued, adult education is a function of the state and is therefore regulated according to certain economic, political, and cultural interests and pressures. Second, as the chapters by Foley, Tett, and Malcolm show, educational institutions are situated in historical and social contexts that suggest that adult education is intimately linked with maintaining particular cultural and social arrangements. Capitalist societies structure these arrangements around inequalities, because capitalism foundationally depends on a labor force of differing levels of skill. Educational institutions, by creating and maintaining a steady supply of workers with these differing levels, ensure that existing and future workforces can adapt to changes in investment, production, and trade circumstances. They do this through complicated systems involving financing, credentialing, selection criteria, curricula, pedagogies, cognitive classification, rewards, and assessment. Thus, by transmitting, sustaining, and legitimizing particular systems of structured inequality, educational systems uphold the characteristics of a particular order of social relations.

Third, adult educators should closely consider class because of how it plays out in everyday educational situations and practices. For example, consider teaching: what educators teach and how they teach are choices made from a wider universe of knowledge and values. Such choices always benefit and privilege some while ignoring, downplaying, or deprivileging others. Curricular and pedagogical choices reflect different ways of understanding and responding to social relations. Fourth, political choices imbricate the adult education profession itself. Consider teaching again: some people are considered worthy or accredited to teach adults; others are not. There are concomitant struggles over autonomy, respect, wages, job security, and evaluation. Educational practices reflect the ways that people and societies think about the transmission of ideologies and cultures. Must we assume that adult educators are always neutral, objective, and benevolent agents of the state? Is their job only to impart basic information necessary for learners to survive and prosper within an economic system? Must it always support a particular social order? Or are there alternative ways to think and behave?

The Practical Importance of Class

Most adult educators assume a very pragmatic orientation, so perhaps it is helpful to think more closely about the links between social class, the everyday educational practices of adult educators, and some of the larger issues that so influence people's attitudes toward education, learning, and society. For me, Myles Horton (quoted in Peters and Bell, 1987, pp. 256–257) best expresses the importance of linking these:

> Things don't operate in a vacuum. They are operating in a given period of history under a given economic system (e.g., capitalism). You have to know where we are in history, in terms of ideas (e.g., democratic ideas, authoritarian ideas). You have to know how they have been carried out by politicians

and industrialists, for example, and what the system has done in the way of structure to affect the people with whom you are working . . . If you want to maximize the control people have over their lives, then you need to know what control they don't have and why.

Such linking of the personal and the social underscores the critical role of adult education. As the great British adult educator R. H. Tawney (1966) indicated, discussions of the role of adult education are really only intelligible in relation to its purposes: they rest on a particular view of people's natures and capabilities and the sort of society that would assist their development. We usually see this notion in discussions about the responsibilities of adult education to encourage greater citizenship and inclusion, topics that are now exercising adult educators the world over (Education and Training for Governance and Active Citizenship in Europe, 2003; Korsgaard, Walters, and Anderson, 2001; Osborne, 1991).

Let's take the example of citizenship and consider how a focus on class might relate to a common adult education activity such as teaching. How and what we teach has a lot to do with our expectations of people and the kinds of citizenship we want to encourage. In a traditional educational approach, ideal citizens come to class, do their assignments on time, obey instructions, conform to the rules, develop a quietly competitive spirit, and generally strive to achieve. They rarely rock the boat, question authority, or think too much for themselves. Outside of educational contexts, ideal citizens voluntarily go to work, do what they're told, and generally refrain from asking awkward questions. Thus, educational institutions serve as places to cultivate the characteristics of passivity, conformity, productivity, and competition. Further and most significantly, they promote the belief that these attributes are always right and proper. So a pedagogic concentration on competition, passivity, and productivity works well to keep the larger social mechanisms of capitalism unexamined.

Yet citizenship can also mean more than passive conformity to what already exists. It can offer the skills, knowledge, and motivation and provide opportunities to challenge and change the status quo for everyone's betterment. So just as educational institutions can inculcate passivity, they can also establish and develop more active citizenship ideals and practices. Indeed, some find that this approach represents one of adult education's imperatives (Foley, 2001). Many educators know that the skills to engage critically in social participation are not ones they received at birth but learned through the practice of active citizenry. Educators encouraging more active citizenship stress that the rights we enjoy now (for example, to vote, to organize, to assemble, to speak freely, to be equal under the law) were not ones that the powerful handed over but rather were ones that we won (and maintain) through thoughtful, reflective, and committed efforts (Milner, 2002).

A class perspective brings such issues into sharper relief; it acknowledges that the structure of societies might be uneven and offers opportunities for action. If educators approach citizenship as a reflection of simple gradations in social strata, they are not likely to encourage resistance or mobilization. Alternatively, if they portray citizenship as part of a hierarchical, value-laden class system based on inequality, then educators and their students can identify notions of injustice and collective grievances and discuss and stimulate possible remedies.

Suggestions for Further Reading

Accepting that adult education is a significant and politicized site in the struggle for knowledge and power requires a candid recognition of the prospects for practice and the opportunity to learn from the rich depictions of previous conflicts. So learning about others who have also explored the links between adult education and social class movements and struggles can provide educators advice and hope. In this final section, I offer some suggestions about further readings that have variously moved, inspired, and energized me into action.

Strong connections between the ideas of adult education, social class, and the broader movements for social change are available in the biographies of Myles Horton (1990), Moses Coady (Welton, 2001), bell hooks (2000), and Paulo Freire (Gadotti, 1994), as well as several of the critical dialogues collected in Torres (1998). Also, in Chapter One I alluded to the work of several critical adult educators from outside North America: Allman (2001), Stromquist (1997), Westwood (Westwood and Thomas, 1991), Thompson (1997, 2000), and Youngman (2000). To these I might add marino (1997), Lovett (1988), Newman (1994, 1999), Mayo (1999), and Holst (2002), each of whom have variously drawn on the traditions of Ettore Gelpi, Eduard Lindeman, N.F.S. Grundtvig, Oskar Negt, Julius Nyerere, Oscar Olsson, and Paulo Freire to provide rich empirical and conceptual studies that connect adult learning and educational practices to the wider interests of class and capitalism. Of course, it is impossible to provide a complete or even a comprehensive list (and my apologies to those I've inadvertently left out), but these authors provide excellent (and readable) places to start.

Discussions of adult education and social class are also found outside of the traditional adult education literature. There are no finer explorations of the historical development of what might be called the working-class tradition of education and adult learning than Simon (1972, 1992) and Rose (2001). More recently, Halsey and colleagues (Halsey, Lauder, Brown, and Wells, 1997) comprehensively explore the centrality of educational policies and practices to capitalism and the functioning of postindustrial societies. Robertson (2000) provides an elegant theoretical and empirical examination of how the changing nature of teachers' work is tied to class, civil society, and wider social formations.

The emergent (at least in the United States) field of working-class studies has also reinvigorated discussion of the intersections of class, adult learning, and institutional practices in North America (Linkon, 1999; Zandy, 2001; Zweig, 2004). Acknowledging that working-class learners now constitute a significant proportion of students enrolled in institutions of higher education, this body of work incorporates a sensitivity to students' working-class roots while suggesting curricular and pedagogic innovations informed by an awareness of class culture. Several recently published books detail the travails of academics from working-class backgrounds (Dews and Law, 1995; Ryan and Sackrey, 1984; Tokarczyk and Fay, 1993). All contain powerful autobiographical and analytic essays that address the personal, professional, and ideological issues in the experiences of working-class teachers and students in higher education. Although it will come as no great shock to most university-based adult educators, "many current higher education practices [still] pose barriers to [adult] participation which include a lack of flexibility in calendar and scheduling, academic content, modes of instruction and availability of learning services" (Commission for a Nation of Lifelong Learners, 1997, p. 3).

Several other higher education studies also provide analyses of how universities treat adult learners from different class backgrounds (Archer, Hutchins, and Ross, 2003; Ball, 2003; Tokarczyk, 2004), how working-class students experience university-level education (Adair and Dahlberg, 2003; Vander Putten, 2001), how university curricula and pedagogy in several disciplines reflect class-based interests (Kumar, 1997; Margolis, 2001), how to challenge the status quo and democratize university classroom practices (Shor, 1992, 1996; Shor and Pari, 2000), and how academic institutions might change to better accommodate the needs and interests of working-class and adult learners (Dunkin and Lindsay, 2001; Knapper and Cropley, 2000; United Nations Educational, Cultural and Scientific Organization, 1998).

These studies all provide a richness of theoretical analysis on class often missing from the field of adult education. For example, many suggest that one issue that many working-class learners experience involves the notion of status incongruity (Sennett and Cobb, 1972), in which the differences between the culture and language of students' working-class backgrounds and the academic environments they enter can create discomfort and uncertainty. Working-class learners can become unsure of their own identity, feel out of place and marginalized, and experience what Ryan and Sackrey (1984, p. 119) tellingly call "the sense of being nowhere at home." Such work also dispels the myth that the working-class pursuit of adult and higher education is always a rejection of or an escape from one's culture and the often harsh and demeaning living and working conditions that shape it. Neither is it, as some maintain, an accommodation to middle-class values or a capitulation to bourgeois cultural hegemony. Rather, it represents for many a telling act of resistance against the repression of a system that does damage to their spirit as well as their bodies (Terkel, 1972). Although for too many working-class learners, education is still "about failure; about being 'found out'" (Reay, 2001, p. 334), it can also provide "a chance for upward mobility [and] a fuller understanding of and interaction with one's self, community and society" (Tokarczyk, 2004, p. 167). Because much of working-class life and culture is already marked by struggle anyway, many working-class learners view their education as a continuance of their personal and collective struggles for a better world—not just for themselves but often for everyone else as well.

Finally, those who wish to further explore the development of class as a concept and its enduring vitality and continued relevance today have a plethora of choices from political, economic, sociological, and historical perspectives. Navigating one's way through such a maze can be disconcerting; Milner (1999) and Seabrook (2002) provide straightforward and cogent guides. Longer introductions to the discourse and language of class are available in Joyce (1995), Savage (2000), and Skeggs (2004). For lucid discussions of the current state of class in the United States, see Aronowitz (2003), Fussell (1992), and Zweig (2004); Curtis, Grabb, and Guppy (1999) offer the same for Canada; and Cannadine (1998) and Roberts (2001) for Great Britain. Finally, three books that spurred me into preparing this sourcebook are Bourdieu and Ferguson (1999), hooks (2000), and Thompson (1997).

In Closing

Many have argued that the idea of class has outlived its usefulness. The complexities of modern society have effaced the antagonisms that Marx described; the word *class* itself has little or no value; the indicators are unreliable (Calvert, 1982). In spite of this, "the fiction that class has ceased to exist is being spread in a world in which inequality has never been greater" (Seabrook, 2002, p. 8). Examining the intersections of class and adult education can alert us to the unexamined patterns of behavior through which society produces and reproduces social classes in the dynamics between educational activities and the wider cultural politics of societies. It can also expose to thoughtful scrutiny the superficiality of a variety of currently prescribed educational reforms: the individualizing of educational opportunities, increased commercial involvement determining educational goals, privatization of schools and colleges, a return to so-called basics, the streaming of learners of all ages into cultural or functional literacies or core competencies, and the increasing pressures to work harder and longer.

To answer the question I posed earlier: I believe that, to be truly effective, adult educators must infuse their work with a critique of capitalism. In so doing, they must expose it not simply as an economic system but rather as a totalizing system of social relations. As educators, they should also resist and challenge (and help others to do so) what Allman (2001, p. 209) calls the postmodern condition: "skepticism, uncertainty, fragmentation, nihilism, and incoherence." This is no easy task. Williams (1961, p. 241) called it the "long revolution": "the systems of meanings and values which a capitalist society has generated has to be defeated in general and in detail by the most sustained kinds of intellectual and educational work."

The totality of capitalism renders it difficult to challenge. However, it also underscores the necessity of doing so if we want to create a fairer and safer world built on more than economic values. Nowadays people often regard approaches that focus on class and other forms of oppression as misguided or even sinister. Instead, some encourage us to accept limited and partial integrations into and accommodations to social orders based on systemic inequalities. Yet we are not bystanders to political contexts but vital and essential members of them. As educators of adults, we have a responsibility to raise important and challenging questions and to build on our students' lived experiences about how inequalities play out in their own lives and workplaces. We must challenge the current directions that capitalist education is taking and resist all attempts to confine adult education to the production and maintenance of human capital. It is my sincere wish that this sourcebook with its claim for the centrality of social class can help us all to do so.

References

Adair, V. C., and Dahlberg, S. L. (eds.). *Reclaiming Class: Women, Poverty, and the Promise of Higher Education in America.* Philadelphia: Temple University Press, 2003.
Allman, P. *Critical Education Against Global Capitalism. Karl Marx and Revolutionary Critical Education.* New York: Bergin & Garvey, 2001.
Apple, M. W. *Ideology and Curriculum.* London: Routledge, 1990.
Apple, M. W. *Education and Power.* London: Routledge, 1995.
Archer, L., Hutchins, M., and Ross, A. (eds.). *Higher Education and Social Class: Issues of Exclusion and Inclusion.* London: Routledge Falmer, 2003.
Aronowitz, S. *How Class Works.* New Haven: Yale University Press, 2003.
Ball, S. *Class Strategies and the Education Market: The Middle Class and Social Advantage.* London: Routledge Falmer, 2003.
Bourdieu, P., and Ferguson, P. P. *The Weight of the World.* Cambridge, England: Polity Press, 1999.
Calvert, P. *The Concept of Class: An Historical Introduction.* London: Hutchinson, 1982.
Cannadine, D. *Class in Britain.* London: Penguin, 1998.
Commission for a Nation of Lifelong Learners. *A Nation Learning: Vision for the Twenty-First Century.* Albany, N.Y.: Regents College, 1997.
Croteau, D. *Politics and the Class Divide.* Philadelphia: Temple University Press, 1995.
Curtis, J., Grabb, E., and Guppy, N. (eds.). *Social Inequality in Canada: Patterns, Problems, and Policies.* Englewood Cliffs, N.J.: Prentice Hall, 1999.
Dews, C.L.B., and Law, C. L. (eds.). *This Fine Place So Far from Home: Voices of Academics from the Working Class.* Philadelphia: Temple University Press, 1995.
Dunkin, R., and Lindsay, A. "Universities as Centers for Lifelong Learning: Opportuni-

ties and Threats at the Institutional Level." In D. Aspin, J. Chapman, M. Hatton, and Y. Sawano (eds.), *International Handbook of Lifelong Learning*. London: Kluwer, 2001. Education and Training for Governance and Active Citizenship in Europe. *Lifelong Learning, Governance, and Active Citizenship in Europe*. Guilford: University of Surrey, 2003.

Foley, G. *Strategic Learning: Understanding and Facilitating Workplace Change*. Sydney: UTS Centre for Popular Education, 2001.

Fussell, P. *Class: A Guide through the American Status System*. New York: Touchstone, 1992.

Gadotti, M. *Reading Paulo Freire: His Life and Work*. (J. Milton, trans.) Albany: State University of New York Press, 1994.

Halsey, A. H., Lauder, H., Brown, P., and Wells, A. S. (eds.). *Education: Culture, Economy, Society*. Oxford: Oxford University Press, 1997.

Holst, J. D. *Social Movements, Civil Society, and Radical Adult Education*. New York: Bergin & Garvey, 2002.

hooks, b. *Where We Stand: Class Matters*. New York: Routledge, 2000.

Horton, M., with Kohl, J., and Kohl, H. *The Long Haul*. New York: Doubleday, 1990.

Joyce, P. (ed.). *Class*. Oxford: Oxford University Press, 1995.

Knapper, C. K., and Cropley, A. J. *Lifelong Learning in Higher Education*. London: Kogan Page, 2000.

Korsgaard, O., Walters, S., and Anderson, R. (eds.). *Learning for Democratic Citizenship*. Copenhagen: Danish National Library of Education, 2001.

Kumar, A. (ed.). *Class Issues: Pedagogy, Cultural Studies, and the Public Sphere*. New York: New York University Press, 1997.

Linkon, S. L. (ed.). *Teaching Working Class*. Amherst: University of Massachusetts Press, 1999.

Lovett, T. (ed.). *Radical Approaches to Adult Education: A Reader*. London: Routledge, 1988.

Margolis, E. (ed.). *The Hidden Curriculum in Higher Education*. New York: Routledge, 2001.

marino, d. *Wild Garden: Art, Education, and the Culture of Resistance*. Toronto: Between the Lines Press, 1997.

Mayo, P. *Gramsci, Freire, and Adult Education: Possibilities for Transformative Action*. London: Zed Books, 1999.

Milner, A. *Class*. London: Sage, 1999.

Milner, H. *Civic Literacy: How Informed Citizens Make Democracy Work*. Hanover: Tufts University Press, 2002.

Newman, M. *Defining the Enemy: Adult Education in Social Action*. Paddington, Australia: Stewart Victor, 1994.

Newman, M. *Maeler's Regard: Images of Adult Learning*. Paddington, Australia: Stewart Victor, 1999.

Offe, C. "New Social Movements: Challenging the Boundaries of Institutional Politics." *Social Research*, 1985, 52, 817–868.

Osborne, K. *Teaching for Democratic Citizenship*. Toronto: Our Schools/Our Selves, 1991.

Peters, J. M., and Bell, B. "Horton of Highlander." In P. Jarvis (ed.), *Twentieth Century Thinkers in Adult Education*. London: Routledge, 1987.

Reay, D. "Finding or Losing Yourself? Working-Class Relationships to Education." *Journal of Education Policy*, 2001, 16(4), 333–346.

Roberts, K. *Class in Modern Britain*. New York: Palgrave, 2001.

Robertson, S. L. *A Class Act*. New York: Falmer Press, 2000.

Rose, J. *The Intellectual Life of the British Working Classes*. New Haven, Conn.: Yale University Press, 2001.

Ryan, J., and Sackrey, C. *Strangers in Paradise: Academics from the Working Class*. Boston: South End Press, 1984.

Savage, M. *Class Analysis and Social Transformation*. Buckingham: Open University Press, 2000.

Seabrook, J. *The No-Nonsense Guide to Class, Caste and Hierarchies*. Oxford: New Internationalist Publications, 2002.

Sennett, R. *The Corrosion of Character*. New York: Norton, 1999.

Sennett, R., and Cobb, J. *The Hidden Injuries of Class*. New York: Vintage, 1972.

Shor, I. *Empowering Education: Critical Teaching for Social Change*. Chicago: University of Chicago Press, 1992.

Shor, I. *When Students have Power: Negotiating Authority in a Critical Pedagogy*. Chicago: University of Chicago Press, 1996.

Shor, I., and Pari, C. (eds.). *Education Is Politics*. Portsmouth, N.H.: Boynton/Cook, 2000.

Simon, B. (ed.). *The Radical Tradition of Education in Britain*. London: Lawrence and Wishart, 1972.

Simon, B. (ed.). *The Search for Enlightenment: The Working Class and Adult Education in the Twentieth Century*. London: Lawrence and Wishart, 1992.

Skeggs, B. *Class, Self, Culture*. London: Routledge, 2004.

Stromquist, N. P. *Literacy for Citizenship*. Albany, N.Y.: SUNY Press, 1997.

Tawney, R. H. *The Radical Tradition: Twelve Essays on Politics, Education and Literature*. Harmondsworth, England: Penguin, 1966.

Terkel, S. *Working*. New York: Avon Books, 1972.

Thompson, J. *Words in Edgeways: Radical Learning for Social Change*. Leicester, England: National Institute of Adult Continuing Education, 1997.

Thompson, J. *Women, Class and Education*. New York: Routledge, 2000.

Tokarczyk, M. M. "Promises to Keep: Working-Class Students and Higher Education." In M. Zweig (ed.), *What's Class Got to Do with It?* Ithaca, N.Y.: Cornell University Press, 2004.

Tokarczyk, M. M., and Fay, E. A. (eds.). *Working-Class Women in the Academy: Laborers in the Knowledge Factory*. Amherst: University of Massachusetts Press, 1993.

Torres, C. A. *Education, Power, and Personal Biography: Dialogues with Critical Educators*. London: Routledge, 1998.

United Nations Educational, Cultural and Scientific Organization (UNESCO). *The Mumbai Statement on Lifelong Learning, Active Citizenship, and the Reform of Higher Education*. Hamburg: UNESCO Institute of Education, 1998.

Vander Putten, J. "Bringing Social Class to the Diversity Challenge." *About Campus*, 2001, 6(5), 14–19.

Welton, M. R. *Little Mosie from the Margaree*. Toronto: Thompson Educational, 2001.

Westwood, S., and Thomas, J. E. (eds.). *Radical Agendas? The Politics of Adult Education*. London: National Institute of Adult Continuing Education, 1991.

Williams, R. *The Long Revolution*. London: Chatto and Windus, 1961.

Youngman, F. *The Political Economy of Adult Education*. London: Zed Books, 2000.

Zandy, J. (ed.). *What We Hold in Common: An Introduction to Working-class Studies*. New York: Feminist Press at CUNY, 2001.

Zweig, M. (ed.). *What's Class Got to Do with It?* Ithaca, N.Y.: Cornell University Press, 2004.

TOM NESBIT *is director of the Centre for Integrated and Credit Studies and associate dean of continuing studies at Simon Fraser University in Vancouver, British Columbia.*

INDEX

Abrahams, D., 56
Adair, V. C., 88
Addison, A., 33
Adult education: barriers to, 24; businesses' interest in, 19; creation of, 73; dependence on capitalism, 75; goals of, 83; history of, 73–74; importance of, 11, 12, 17–18; participation in, 11; role of, 86; structure of, 84–85; struggle for power in, 83; and study of historical perspectives, 50–51. *See also* Education
Adult education policy: and class politics breakdown, 16–17; effect of, on classrooms, 46; factors affecting, 18; global trends affecting, 17–23; goal of, 27; in Nordic countries, 22–23; overview of, 15
African Americans, 79
African National Congress (ANC), 56–57, 60
Aldridge, F., 11
Allman, P., 12, 13, 75, 87, 90
Altenbaugh, R. J., 40
Althusser, L., 5
American Council on Education, 64
ANC. *See* African National Congress (ANC)
Anderson, M. L., 76
Anderson, R., 86
Another World Is Possible (McNally), 67
Antiracism education, 77–78
Apartheid, 57, 58–59
Apple, M. W., 10, 84
Archer, L., 27, 88
Aristocracy, 8
Arkansas, 79
Aronowitz, S., 89
Aronson, A., 70
Assessment, 32
Authentic activities, 29–30

Badat, S., 55, 57, 60
Bakan, J., 80
Ball, M., 40
Ball, S., 88
Banal, R., 24
Bannerji, B., 76, 77
Barton, D., 28

Beck, U., 17, 21, 23, 24
Beck-Gernsheim, E., 17, 21, 23, 24
Beeghley, E. L., 9
Bell, B., 85
Black Consciousness Movement, 59
Blair, T., 28
Bok, M., 22
Border Country (Williams), 43
Bourdieu, P., 8, 89
Bourgeoisie, 7
Bowles, S., 10
Bridge programs, 64–65
Brooks, J., 67, 70
Brown, P., 87
Business sector interests, 19
Butterwick, S., 75

Calliste, A., 76
Calvert, P., 89
Canada, 22, 47, 76–77
Capital investments, 68–69
Capitalism: dependence of adult education on, 75; effects of, 6; extractive, 69; interest of, in education, 10–11; and patriarchy, 67; power of, 80; reproduction of, 75; requirements of, 10, 74; social classes in, 6; as source of racism, 80; theoretical debates regarding, 74
Care-taking tasks, 65–66, 68–70
Cavanagh, J., 69
Cayetano, F., 67, 70
Chicago, 64
Chua, A., 80
Citizenship, 86
Clark, T. N., 16, 23
Class. *See* Social class
Class analysis: lack of, in literature, 11–12; principles of, 9–10; questions raised by, 10
Class consciousness, 43
Class perspective, 84–85
Class politics, breakdown of, 16–17
Class struggles, effects of, 75
Classrooms: effect of policies on, 46; making class visible in, 49–52; tools for transforming racial practices in, 79–81
Clover, D., 55

93

Giddens, A., 20
Gintis, H., 10
Giroux, H., 34
Global capitalism, 19
Goldberg, D. T., 79
Gowen, S., 39
Grabb, E., 89
Gramsci, A., 5
Griffin, C., 21
Griffin, S. M., 77
Group Areas Act, 59
Gruppy, N., 89
Gustavsson, B., 24

Habermas, J., 5, 6
Hagstrom, W. O., 12
Hahnel, R., 64
Hall, B., 55
Halsey, A. H., 34, 87
Hamilton, M., 28
Hampton, W., 40
Handbook of Adult and Continuing Education (Merriam and Cunningham; Wilson and Hayes), 11
Harding, S., 78
Hart, M., 3, 63
Hayes, E. R., 11, 75
Head, D., 40
Heath, S. B., 33
Hegemony, 5
Highlander Education and Research Center, 40
History, 49–51
HIV/AIDS, 56
Hochschild, A. R., 69, 70
Holst, J. D., 87
hooks, b., 11, 76, 83, 87, 89
Horton, M., 40, 87
Hutchins, M., 27, 88

Identities, 66–67
Identity politics, 9
IMF. *See* International Monetary Fund (IMF)
India, 60
Individualization: and class politics breakdown, 17; European policies affecting, 23; focus on, 28; and students' view of failure, 48
Industrialization, 7, 8, 73
Institutions, 37, 85
International Monetary Fund (IMF), 65, 69

Ismail, S., 53–54, 60

Jamison, A., 54–55, 55, 60
Jefferson School of Social Science, 40
Jensen, R., 76
Johnson, A. F., 18
Johnson, R., 34
Johnson-Bailey, J., 75
Joyce, P., 89

Kincheloe, J. L., 11
King, J. E., 64
Knapper, C. K., 88
Knowledge: generation of, 60; purpose of, 35
Korpi, W., 15
Korsgaard, O., 86
Korten, D. C., 66, 69
Kumar, A., 88

Labor market changes, 64
Lange, E. A., 66
Language: critical awareness of, 31, 32–33; of home and community versus school, 32–34
Lauder, H., 87
Law, C. L., 88
Leach, L., 37
Learning: common view of, 29; deficit view of, 28; purpose of, 35; responsibility for, 20–21, 48; in social movements, 55–56
Learning styles, of working class, 39–43
Lenin, V., 74
Letters, 32
Liberation, 17
Lifelong learning: and adult education policy changes, 18–23; barriers to, 18–19, 21; benefits of, 18; EU's definition of, 21; EU's goals for, 20, 27–28; importance of, 18; individual nature of, 20–21; new economy perspective of, 19–20; past focus on, 18; and policy expectations, 27; and power, 34; working-class society's view of, 28
Lindsay, A., 88
Linkon, S. L., 68, 83, 88
Lipset, S. M., 16, 23
Lisbon European Council, 20
Literacy: common view of, 29; definition of, 28–29; and power, 34
Literacy programs: assessment in, 32; curriculum in, 29–30; effects of,

Back Issue/Subscription Order Form

Copy or detach and send to:

Jossey-Bass, A Wiley Company, 989 Market Street, San Francisco CA 94103-1741

Call or fax toll-free: Phone 888-378-2537 6:30AM – 3PM PST; Fax 888-481-2665

Back Issues: Please send me the following issues at $29 each
(Important: please include series initials and issue number, such as ACE96.)

_____

_____

_____

$ _____   Total for single issues

$ _____   SHIPPING CHARGES: SURFACE   Domestic   Canadian

		Domestic	Canadian
	First Item	$5.00	$6.00
	Each Add'l Item	$3.00	$1.50

For next-day and second-day delivery rates, call the number listed above.

Subscriptions: Please __start __renew my subscription to *New Directions for Adult and Continuing Education* for the year 2____ at the following rate:

U.S.	__Individual $80	__Institutional $170
Canada	__Individual $80	__Institutional $210
All Others	__Individual $104	__Institutional $244

**For more information about online subscriptions visit
www.interscience.wiley.com**

$ _____   Total single issues and subscriptions (Add appropriate sales tax for your state for single issue orders. No sales tax for U.S. subscriptions. Canadian residents, add GST for subscriptions and single issues.)

__Payment enclosed (U.S. check or money order only)

__VISA __MC __AmEx #_____ Exp. Date _____

Signature _____ Day Phone _____

__ Bill Me (U.S. institutional orders only. Purchase order required.)

Purchase order # _____

Federal Tax ID13559302   **GST 89102 8052**

Name _____

Address _____

_____

Phone _____ E-mail _____

For more information about Jossey-Bass, visit our Web site at www.josseybass.com

education—whether established or emerging—provide insights into what it means to be critical and how it affects the concrete practices of teaching adults. Chapter topics include critical theory, feminism, critical postmodernism, Africentrism, queer theory, and cultural studies.
ISBN 0-7879-7590-7

ACE101 **Adult Education in an Urban Context: Problems, Practices, and Programming for Inner-City Communities**
Larry G. Martin, Elice E. Rogers
This sourcebook offers adult education scholars and practitioners in academic, community, and work-related urban settings insight into the education and learning problems and needs confronted by low-income residents of inner-city communities. Additionally, it offers fresh perspectives and approaches to practice that can assist these residents in crossing the socioeconomic and race-ethnicity borders that separate them from more affluent urban communities.
ISBN 0-7879-7433-1

ACE100 **Facilitating Learning in Online Environments**
Steven R. Aragon
Presents models, methods, and strategies that facilitate and promote learning within online environments. Arguing that success in online environments is dependent on the role of autonomy in order to create sustained and enduring learners, contributors demonstrate how quality online programs are made up of a "blend" of technology, pedogogy, organization, strategy, and vision; explore the concept of online social presence as a significant factor in improving instructional effectiveness and contributing to a feeling of community among learners; and offer strategies for instructors facing the new challenges and opportunities of the online educational experience.
ISBN 0-7879-7268-1

ACE99 **Environmental Adult Education: Ecological Learning, Theory, and Practice for Socio-Environmental Change**
Darlene E. Clover, Lilian H. Hill
Situates environmental adult education within a socio-political and eco-epistemological framework, explores how new language and metaphors can counteract problematic modern worldviews, and analyzes the potential of environmental, justice-based learning to combat socio-environmental oppressions. It provides effective ways educators can connect social and ecological issues in their educational work in community, classroom, or social movements.
ISBN 0-7879-7170-7

ACE98 **New Perspectives on Designing and Implementing Professional Development of Teachers of Adults**
Kathleen P. King, Patricia A. Lawler
Explores how to make professional development more pertinent by looking at teachers of adults as adult learners themselves. It also presents an astute vision of current needs and trends, theory, and recommended practice to guide professional development in the many contexts in which teachers of adults work today—from higher education to adult literacy to corporate training.
ISBN 0-7879-6918-4

ACE97 Accelerated Learning for Adults: The Promise and Practice of Intensive
Educational Formats
Raymond J. Wlodkowski, Carol E. Kasworm
The first major publication that addresses the current practice and research
of accelerated learning formats in higher education. Contributors explore the
scope of accelerated learning as it is practiced today and offer practitioner
guidelines and insights for best practices in program and course design,
learning strategies, and assessment approaches, as well as the integration of
distance learning and service-learning into accelerated learning programs.
ISBN 0-7879-6794-7

ACE96 Learning and Sociocultural Contexts: Implications for Adults,
Community, and Workplace Education
Mary V. Alfred
Understanding how sociocultural contexts shape the learning experience is
crucial to designing, implementing, and facilitating effective learning
activities with and for adults. This volume explores some of the contexts
within which learning occurs and the social and cultural dynamics that
influence learning and teaching. The contributors' aim is to create an
awareness of the importance of context in adult learning and to encourage
adult educators to be reflective of their practice, to understand how social
and cultural contexts influence classroom dynamics, and to take critical
action to ameliorate hegemonic practices in adult education.
ISBN 0-7879-6326-7

ACE95 Adult Learning in Community
Susan Imel, David Stein
Explores how adult learning occurs in naturally forming communities. As
illustrated by the chapters in this volume, this learning takes a variety of
forms, and in a variety of locations. It is characterized by individuals coming
together to exercise control and influence over the direction, content, and
purposes of their learning and emphasizes the community or social as
opposed to the individual level of learning. Although many learning
communities are homogeneous in nature, several chapters reveal how power
and politics play a role as well as how the presence of a facilitator can change
the dynamic.
ISBN 0-7879-6323-2

ACE94 Collaborative Inquiry as a Strategy for Adult Learning
Lyle Yorks, Elizabeth Kasl
Examines the practice of collaborative inquiry (CI), a systematic process that
educators can use to help adults make meaning from their experience,
through richly detailed case descriptions. Highlights particular
characteristics of the authors' projects so that this volume, taken as a whole,
represents the diversity of issues important to adult educators. Provides
guidance to adult educators while at the same time adding to the emerging
discourse about this process.
ISBN 0-7879-6322-4

ACE93 Contemporary Viewpoints on Teaching Adults Effectively
Jovita Ross-Gordon
The aim of this sourcebook was to bring together several authors who have
contributed through their recent publications to the recent literature on
effective teaching of adults. Rather than promoting a single view of what

constitutes good teaching of adults, the chapters challenge each of us to reflect on our beliefs regarding teaching and learning along with our understandings of adults learners, the teaching-learning environment, and the broader social context within which adult continuing education takes place.
ISBN 0-7879-6229-5

ACE92   Sociocultural Perspectives on Learning through Work
Tara Fenwick
Offers an introduction to current themes among academic researchers who are interested in sociocultural understandings of work-based learning and working knowledge—how people learn in and through everyday activities that they think of as work. Explores how learning is embedded in the social relationships, cultural dynamics, and politics of work, and they recommend different ways for educators to be part of the process.
ISBN 0-7879-5775-5

ACE91   Understanding and Negotiating the Political Landscape of Adult Education
Catherine A. Hansman, Peggy A. Sissel
Provides key insights into the politics and policy issues in adult education today. Offering effective strategies for reflection and action, chapters explore issues in examination and negotiation of the political aspects of higher education, adult educators in K–12-focused colleges of education, literacy education, social welfare reform, professional organizations, and identity of the field.
ISBN 0-7879-5775-5

ACE90   Promoting Journal Writing in Adult Education
Leona M. English, Marie A. Gillen
Exploring the potential for personal growth and learning through journal writing for student and mentor alike, this volume aims to establish journal writing as an integral part of the teaching and learning process. Offers examples of how journal writing can be, and has been, integrated into educational areas as diverse as health education, higher education, education for women, and English as a Second Language.
ISBN 0-7879-5774-7

ACE89   The New Update on Adult Learning Theory
Sharan B. Merriam
A companion work to 1993's popular *An Update on Adult Learning Theory,* this issue examines the developments, research, and continuing scholarship in self-directed learning. Exploring context-based learning, informal and incidental learning, somatic learning, and narrative learning, the authors analyze recent additions to well-established theories and discuss the potential impact of today's cutting-edge approaches.
ISBN 0-7879-5773-9

ACE88   Strategic Use of Learning Technologies
Elizabeth J. Burge
The contributors draw on case examples to explore the advantages and disadvantages of three existing learning technologies—print, radio, and the Internet—and examine how a large urban university has carefully combined old and new technologies to provide a range of learner services tailored to its enormous and varied student body.
ISBN 0-7879-5426-8

ACE87 Team Teaching and Learning in Adult Education
Mary-Jane Eisen, Elizabeth J. Tisdell
The contributors show how team teaching can increase both organizational
and individual learning in settings outside of a traditional classroom, for
example, a recently deregulated public utility, a national literacy
organization, and community-based settings such as Chicago's south side.
They discuss how team teaching can be used in colleges and universities,
describing strategies for administrators and teachers who want to integrate it
into their curricula and classrooms.
ISBN 0-7879-5425-X

ACE86 Charting a Course for Continuing Professional Education: Reframing
Professional Practice
Vivian W. Mott, Barbara J. Daley
This volume offers a resource to help practitioners examine and improve
professional practice, and set new directions for the field of CPE across
multiple professions. The contributors provide a brief review of the
development of the field of CPE, analyze significant issues and trends that
are shaping and changing the field, and propose a vision of the future of
CPE.
ISBN 0-7879-5424-1

ACE85 Addressing the Spiritual Dimensions of Adult Learning: What Educators
Can Do
Leona M. English, Marie A. Gillen
The contributors discuss how mentoring, self-directed learning, and
dialogue can be used to promote spiritual development, and advocate the
learning covenant as a way of formalizing the sanctity of the bond between
learners and educators. Drawing on examples from continuing professional
education, community development, and health education, they show how a
spiritual dimension has been integrated into adult education programs.
ISBN 0-7879-5364-4

ACE84 An Update on Adult Development Theory: New Ways of Thinking About
the Life Course
M. Carolyn Clark, Rosemary J. Caffarella
This volume presents discussions of well-established theories and new
perspectives on learning in adulthood. Knowles' andragogy, self-directed
learning, Mezirow's perspective transformation, and several other models are
assessed for their contribution to our understanding of adult learning. In
addition, recent theoretical orientations, including consciousness and
learning, situated cognition, critical theory, and feminist pedagogy, are
discussed in terms of how each expands the knowledge base of adult
learning.
ISBN 0-7879-1171-2

ACE83 The Welfare-to-Work Challenge for Adult Literacy Educators
Larry G. Martin, James C. Fisher
Welfare reform and workforce development legislation has had a dramatic
impact on the funding, implementation, and evaluation of adult basic
education and literacy programs. This issue provides a framework for
literacy practitioners to better align their field with the demands of the Work
First environment and to meet the pragmatic expectations of an extended
list of stakeholders.
ISBN 0-7879-1170-4

ACE82   Providing Culturally Relevant Adult Education: A Challenge for the
         Twenty-First Century
         Talmadge C. Guy
         This issue offers more inclusive theories that focus on how learners
         construct meaning in a social and cultural context. Chapters identify ways
         that adult educators can work more effectively with racially, ethnically, and
         linguistically marginalized learners, and explore how adult education can be
         an effective tool for empowering learners to take control of their
         circumstances.
         ISBN 0-7879-1167-4

ACE79   The Power and Potential of Collaborative Learning Partnerships
         Iris M. Saltiel, Angela Sgroi, Ralph G. Brockett
         This volume draws on examples of collaborative partnerships to explore the
         many ways collaboration can generate learning and knowledge. The
         contributors identify the factors that make for strong collaborative
         relationships, and they reveal how these partnerships actually help learners
         generate knowledge and insights well beyond what each brings to the
         learning situation.
         ISBN 0-7879-9815-X

ACE77   Using Learning to Meet the Challenges of Older Adulthood
         James C. Fisher, Mary Alice Wolf
         Combining theory and research in educational gerontology with the practice
         of older adult learning and education, this volume explores issues related to
         older adult education in academic and community settings. It is designed for
         educators and others concerned with the phenomenon of aging in America
         and with the continuing development of the field of educational
         gerontology.
         ISBN 0-7879-1164-X

ACE75   Assessing Adult Learning in Diverse Settings: Current Issues and
         Approaches
         Amy D. Rose, Meredyth A. Leahy
         Examines assessment approaches analytically from different programmatic
         levels and looks at the implications of these differing approaches. Chapters
         discuss the implications of cultural differences as well as ideas about
         knowledge and knowing and the implications these ideas can have for both
         the participant and the program.
         ISBN 0-7879-9840-0

ACE70   A Community-Based Approach to Literacy Programs: Taking Learners'
         Lives into Account
         Peggy A. Sissel
         Encouraging a community-based approach that takes account of the reality
         of learner's lives, this volume offers suggestions for incorporating knowledge
         about a learner's particular context, culture, and community into adult
         literacy programming.
         ISBN 0-7879-9867-2

ACE69   What Really Matters in Adult Education Program Planning: Lessons in
         Negotiating Power and Interests
         Ronald M. Cervero, Arthur L. Wilson
         Identifies issues faced by program planners in practice settings and the
         actual negotiation strategies they use. Argues that planning is generally

conducted within a set of personal, organizational, and social relationships among people who may have similar, different, or conflicting interests and the program planner's responsibility centers on how to negotiate these interests to construct an effective program.
ISBN 0-7879-9866-4

ACE66   **Mentoring: New Strategies and Challenges**
Michael W. Galbraith, Norman H. Cohen
Assists educators in clarifying and describing various elements of the mentoring process. Also intended to enhance the reader's understanding of the utility, practice application, and research potential of mentoring in adult and continuing education.
ISBN 0-7879-9912-1

ACE59   **Applying Cognitive Learning Theory to Adult Learning**
Daniele D. Flannery
While much is written about adult learning, basic tenets of cognitive theory are often taken for granted. This volume presents an understanding of basic cognitive theory and applies it to the teaching-learning exchange.
ISBN 1-55542-716-2

ACE57   **An Update on Adult Learning Theory**
Sharan B. Merriam
This volume presents discussions of well-established theories and new perspectives on learning in adulthood. Knowles' andragogy, self-directed learning, Mezirow's perspective transformation, and several other models are assessed for their contribution to our understanding of adult learning.
ISBN 1-55542-684-0

**NEW DIRECTIONS FOR
ADULT AND CONTINUING EDUCATION
IS NOW AVAILABLE ONLINE AT WILEY INTERSCIENCE**

What is Wiley InterScience?

Wiley InterScience is the dynamic online content service from John Wiley & Sons delivering the full text of over 300 leading scientific, technical, medical, and professional journals, plus major reference works, the acclaimed *Current Protocols* laboratory manuals, and even the full text of select Wiley print books online.

What are some special features of Wiley InterScience?

Wiley InterScience Alerts is a service that delivers table of contents via e-mail for any journal available on Wiley InterScience as soon as a new issue is published online.
Early View is Wiley's exclusive service presenting individual articles online as soon as they are ready, even before the release of the compiled print issue. These articles are complete, peer-reviewed, and citable.
CrossRef is the innovative multi-publisher reference linking system enabling readers to move seamlessly from a reference in a journal article to the cited publication, typically located on a different server and published by a different publisher.

How can I access Wiley InterScience?

Visit http://www.interscience.wiley.com

Guest Users can browse Wiley InterScience for unrestricted access to journal Tables of Contents and Article Abstracts, or use the powerful search engine.
Registered Users are provided with a *Personal Home Page* to store and manage customized alerts, searches, and links to favorite journals and articles. Additionally, Registered Users can view free Online Sample Issues and preview selected material from major reference works.
Licensed Customers are entitled to access full-text journal articles in PDF, with select journals also offering full-text HTML.

How do I become an Authorized User?

Authorized Users are individuals authorized by a paying Customer to have access to the journals in Wiley InterScience. For example, a university that subscribes to Wiley journals is considered to be the Customer. Faculty, staff and students authorized by the university to have access to those journals in Wiley InterScience are Authorized Users. Users should contact their Library for information on which Wiley journals they have access to in Wiley InterScience.

ASK YOUR INSTITUTION ABOUT WILEY INTERSCIENCE TODAY!